A DRUG
FOR THE
DEPRESSED
AND THE
INSANE

STEPHAN HESS

A DEVOTIONAL
FOR THE
DEPRESSED AND
THE INSANE

A DEVOTIONAL FOR THE DEPRESSED AND THE INSANE

Stephan Hess

authorHOUSE®

AuthorHouse™
1663 Liberty Drive
Bloomington, IN 47403
www.authorhouse.com
Phone: 1-800-839-8640

First published by AuthorHouse   08/09/2011

ISBN: 978-1-4634-3103-7 (sc)
ISBN: 978-1-4634-3104-4 (ebk)

Library of Congress Control Number: 2011911555

Printed in the United States of America

FORWARD

"A Devotional for the Depressed and the Insane" is simply meant to raise questions that will take the reader to an outward place; to a new and, hopefully, engaging vantage point.

This is a devotional written with a thought and a heart toward folks that are troubled and depressed and, perhaps, a little mentally imbalanced.

It is a lay work; I'm making no pretensions. But it is also a reaching-out sort of meditation, to walk though the year with. Numbered but not dated so it that it can be picked up and used at any time, set aside and then picked up again without having to track down where one has been with regard to a calendar. Keeping things simple . . .

*   *   *

Paul, being interviewed in Athens, said to the rulers and the philosophers, **" . . . I found an altar with this inscription, TO THE UNKNOWN GOD, Whom therefore ye ignorantly worship, him I declare unto you."** . . .

. . . Knowing and not knowing are often viewpoints not far from eachother. Paul implies that the "unknowable" is now "knowable": he stood knowing a few feet from those who did not know. So maybe depression and mental illness, at least in some cases, are just steps away from joy and harmony.

The questions are not intended to be leading, though some may appear to be. The biblical verses are, after all, from a spiritual text. As a consequence, like most spiritual documents, they have their own purpose and direction, which isn't necessarily a bad thing. But the answers are the individual reader's answers. Don't allow yourself to be proselytized. Maybe you should get angry at the questions. But never stay where you are. It's not a matter of right or wrong answers. They should be honest answers, though. And each honest answer might be like taking a step: away from . . . and going to.

This isn't about finding religion or spirituality. It's about helping someone in finding their way out. Let the questions cause you to look around; let them be a part of your first step out of depression and whatever else you may be struggling with . . . if you are struggling with anything. And if you take that first step out of yourself, keep on going . . . to where ever you're going.

A note on the biblical entries: I use two versions. One is the Authorized Version **(AV)**, the good old King James, because it's classic and, sometimes, fun. The other is the In Your Face Version **(iffy)**, because it's non-classic and it is fun, too.

SH

Day 1

Matthew 18:2-4 **Jesus called forward a little child and sat him in the middle of his disciples. He said to them,**
"This is the truth, except if you will be changed to become like the little children you will find no place for yourselves in the kingdom of heaven.
Who is the greater in the kingdom of heaven?
It is that person who will be as humble as this little child."—(iffy)

Questions:

Can you find a place without trouble and contention in your heart?

Is your need the need of an adult? . . . or do you need to be loved as a little child is loved?

NOTES/THOUGHTS:

Day 2

Philippians 2:1 **Have you gotten anything from Jesus'
love?
Have you been encouraged by him?
Do you think you've been touched by his Holy
Spirit; maybe even so much that you're kinder
and more caring?**—(iffy)

Questions:

The kind acts of Jesus . . . are they seeds that might be
planted in your heart?

Have you clearly heard of the things that Jesus was supposed
to have done?

NOTES/THOUGHTS:

Day 3

Philippians 2:7 **But [Jesus] just became a nobody, like a day laborer or a carwash attendant, he became very human.**—(iffy)

Questions:

Do you think that Jesus wants to be better than you?

Do you think that you're less than Jesus?

NOTES/THOUGHTS:

Day 4

Philippians 2:14,15 **Complaints and arguments you can
do without, you are children of God and these
times of uncaring and anger need to see the
life of God through you who are his bright and
shining stars!**—(iffy)

There's a path through the darkest of places,
it is a living love that resonates
in the quietness of the hollow hills,
at the end it lifts up the wanderer
who's now found home in the presence of Christ.

Question:

Have you looked to see if there's a glow in your heart?

NOTES/THOUGHTS:

Day 5

1 John 4:6 **We belong to God, he calls us his own
children.
Those who know him respond to us; those who
don't know him tend to ignore us.
From this we learn something: Where God is in
others and where he is not.**—(iffy)

Questions:

How do other folks look at you? . . . what is in their faces?

How do you look at other folks? . . . what do they see in
your face?

NOTES/THOUGHTS:

Day 6

1 John 4:7 **My friends! We must always follow the path of loving one another.**
Love comes from God. That love in our lives shows our birth in Christ!
That love in our lives is our friendship with God.—(iffy)

Questions:

Do you think about love?

Have you ever thought about what it means to walk in love?

Are you loved?

Are you willing to love?

NOTES/THOUGHTS:

Day 7

Proverbs 27:8 **The unsettled heart ignores its home and is like a bird flitting from branch to branch.**—(iffy)

Questions:

Will you find peace by pacing back and forth?

Do you think it is possible to stop and let God touch your heart? . . . do you think he can, or can't?

NOTES/THOUGHTS:

Day 8

1 Corinthians 1:25 **God's foolishness stands much higher than the calculated wisdom of human beings. God's flaws (even in reproach and defeat) are impenetrable to the greatest capacity of humanity's powers.**—(iffy)

Where is the answer from our simple minds
to the alpine flowers on the mountain,
poised to bow before the winds of Autumn?
Yet, in their season, they raise in the Sun
what they have gotten from the hands of God.

Question:

Is it in the mind, or is it in the heart that one can really appreciate the glory of such things?

NOTES/THOUGHTS:

Day 9

Psalm 119:72 **All success and wealth I see here [oh God] fade when you speak.**—(iffy)

Values I follow
will they change in the conflict?
My heart beats the same.

Questions:

How does one succeed?

Is there an overriding principle?

And . . . is it worth it?

NOTES/THOUGHTS:

Day 10

Genesis 4:9 **"Am I my brother's caretaker?"**—(iffy)

<u>Questions:</u>

Did he [Cain] just answer his own question?

Do you, do I, look like our brother's or sister's caretaker?

NOTES/THOUGHTS:

Day 11

Exodus 2:22 **"Have I become a stranger in a strange land, a person without a home?"**—(iffy)

Questions:

What causes that sense of "alone-ness"?

How can one reach out from that sense of "alone-ness"?

NOTES/THOUGHTS:

Day 12

Exodus 31:3 **"I [God] have placed in you my Spirit of wisdom, understanding and knowledge to craft and to forge a positive life.**
Through your hands and through your life the creative mind of God is revealed."—(iffy)

Question:

Is God struggling to reach out through you?

NOTES/THOUGHTS:

Day 13

Exodus 34:29 **When Moses came down from the mountain, after talking with God and receiving the Law, he did not know that his appearance was transformed.**—(iffy)

Questions:

Where have you been today?

How do you look?

NOTES/THOUGHTS:

Day 14

Leviticus 6:13 **"Keep the fire burning on the altar, never let it go out."**—(iffy)

The place that is before the throne of God
for the atonement and reparation,
mercy in the face of wrongs committed.
The place where the fire is always burning.

Questions:

Aren't we supposed to attend to that altar?

Is your fire burning?

NOTES/THOUGHTS:

Day 15

John 6:28,29 **"Well," they asked Jesus, "what's there for us to do that's the work of God?"**
And Jesus replied, "Put your complete trust and confidence in the one whom God has sent."—(iffy)

Jesus is asked about a course of action.
But he appears to direct that question
toward the putting on of an attitude.

Question:

What does that say about "the work of God"?

NOTES/THOUGHTS:

Day 16

John 7:37,38 **On the last day of the festival, Jesus call out, standing,**
"If anyone thirsts, I will quench your thirst; you can always come to me.
The scriptures say that anyone who believes in me, 'Rivers of living water will surge out from the core of your being.'"—(iffy)

He gives to our need
and his life rushes through us.
Rivers to forests.

Question:

Have you simply walked over to Jesus and asked?

NOTES/THOUGHTS:

Day 17

John 8:7 **These [who wanted to stone the woman caught in moral violation] insisted on an answer from Jesus. Finally he stood up and said to them, "Is there any man here who is perfect?**
If there is, then he should throw the first stone."—(iffy)

Questions:

If you were perfect what would you do?

Do you know what Jesus did?

If you know, or find out, then why do you think that Jesus acted in the way that he did?

NOTES/THOUGHTS:

Day 18

John 8:12 **Jesus again spoke, "I am the light of the world.**
The one who follows me will not have a dark path to walk on, that person's life will be filled with light!"—(iffy)

Sunlight on a road
is like an illumined map.
Christ is just ahead.

Questions:

What Jesus claims, does it challenge what we know?..or have been told?

Does, perhaps, what Jesus claims challenge us to do something about it?

NOTES/THOUGHTS:

Day 19

Job 24:1 **Why, seeing times are not hidden from the Almighty, do they that know him not see his days?**—(AV)

<u>Question:</u>

If God loves us so much why don't we have access to all that he sees, knows and does?

NOTES/THOUGHTS:

Day 20

Proverbs 14:11 **Not one portion of the house of the wicked will be left standing.**
Yet one who stands upright before God will dwell in a tent of sanctuary and growth.—(iffy)

Questions:

How do you appear before God?

When you look in the mirror, what is it that you see?

What is "sanctuary" for you?

NOTES/THOUGHTS:

Day 21

Proverbs 26:20 **No fuel, no fire, it ceases: if there's no one to tell a rumor, or pass a little gossip along, conflict and hard feelings just fade away.**—(iffy)

Kindly silence comes,
more comfort than many words.
A smile soothes the tears.

Questions:

Do you talk just to pass the time away? . . . or do you have a purpose in mind?

Where is your heart when your mouth opens?

NOTES/THOUGHTS:

Day 22

Luke 12:31,32 **"Seek for all that is of God and he will respond in kind and take care of you.**
There's only a few of you, but there's nothing to be afraid of.
The kingdom is yours!
God, your father, is pleased to give it to you."—(iffy)

Question:

In what directions have you turned and still haven't quite found that "one thing" that gives rest to that restless, searching part of your being?

NOTES/THOUGHTS:

Day 23

Psalm 84:2 **My soul longeth, yea, even fainteth for the courts of the Lord: my heart and my flesh crieth out for the living God.**—(AV)

Question:

A place where we're wanted and loved . . . wouldn't it be nice to be there?

NOTES/THOUGHTS:

Day 24

Matthew 18:20 **For where two or three are gathered together in my name, there am I in the midst of them.**—(AV)

Clasped hands have purpose.
A knot tied is by design . . .
Strong even in rest.

Questions:

What is the NOW of Christ?

Where is he?

NOTES/THOUGHTS:

Day 25

Matthew 20:16 **"The first are many, the last are few.**
Those who stand to heed the call are chosen.
Those who endure to the end are victorious,
firstplace.
It's not who starts, it's who finishes.
There's no secondplace."—(iffy)

It's not for your skills,
it's for you to just say, yes.
He loves you that much.

Questions:

What is the call of Christ?

Is it for your skills or capabilities?

Or does he call you for some other reason?

NOTES/THOUGHTS:

Day 26

Hebrews 11:1 **Faith is now the confidence in the reality of what is hoped for, it is the living demonstration of that which is unseeable.**—(iffy)

Questions:

Can one live, really LIVE, in hope?

How can you have confidence in that which is not seen?

NOTES/THOUGHTS:

Day 27

Hebrews 11:3 **God spoke and the worlds were made;
it is through faith that we perceive this.
And so we now see what was created by whom
we don't see.**—(iffy)

Questions:

Are you living in and around "the unknown"?

Also, could it be that the greatest dynamic in the Universe
is unobtainable except by faith?

NOTES/THOUGHTS:

Day 28

Hebrews 12:14 **With everyone and with God we should proceed with peace.**
No one sees God without this peace.—(iffy)

<u>Questions:</u>

If you were to have a daily conversation with God, could you continue unchanged? . . . or do you think you would eventually walk away?

NOTES/THOUGHTS:

Day 29

Hebrews 13:8 **Jesus Christ the same yesterday, and today, and forever.**—(AV)

Question:

Is faith really for all seasons and situations?

NOTES/THOUGHTS:

Day 30

James 1:2-4 **My family, joyously regard the moments when various trials come to greet you.**
Know that this attack on your faith builds patience.
Yet patience is built with skill, and it is in you that this is working, perfecting faith, completing the character for one who will lack in nothing.—(iffy)

No one wants trouble.
But trouble will come our way.
Who comes? Friend or foe?

Questions:

Are there patterns in our lives that we can re-shape to change outcomes?

Just as importantly, are there patterns in our hearts that need to be re-shaped regardless of the outcomes?

NOTES/THOUGHTS:

Day 31

Hebrews 13:13 **Let's step outside the box, because Jesus is out there waiting for us, and let's be willing to take upon ourselves the disapproval directed torward him.**—(iffy)

Christ takes us away,
leading us from what we know,
into a new land.

Questions:

How "big" is the place where you are, right now?

How small is the horizon at the end of the road that you choose to follow?

NOTES/THOUGHTS:

Day 32

James 1:27 **What is the value of religion that's pure?**
   This is the value:
   It stands before God the Father by kneeling to the
   needs of those absolutely forlorn and destitute,
   the abandoned and the grieving; but it does not
   yield an inch to cynicism, nor to anger.—(iffy)

Unquenchable love;
how to express such a thing.
But does it exist?

Questions:

Can "religion" be so incorrupt?

How could you, how could I, walk through the harshness of
reality with untarnished hearts and attitudes?

NOTES/THOUGHTS:

Day 33

Matthew 11:28-30 **"You can come to me if you're weary and burnt out;**
I will give you rest. Serve with me and learn from me.
Gentleness and humility are in my heart, and with me your heart will find peace and rest.
Also, it is easy to serve with me, because you'll find that no burden is ever taken on alone."—(iffy)

Who offers the kind hand in weariness?
Around me with speeding purpose all pass on,
away from my pleading and broken heart.
I am unravelled and directionless.
Can one someone come by and say, "Hello"?

Questions:

What does your heart need, right now?

What are you crying out for?

NOTES/THOUGHTS:

Day 34

Deuteronomy 30:14 **"God's word is very close to you, it is in your mouth and it is in your heart so that you may act on it!"**—(iffy)

<u>Question:</u>

Could what God speaks into your heart become an essential part of your daily life? . . . why, or why not?

NOTES/THOUGHTS:

Day 35

Deuteronomy 29:29 **"What hasn't been revealed to us, well, that's God's business.**
But what has been shown to us is ours, and it's ours to share so that all might benefit and live through what has been revealed."—(iffy)

There are many mysteries before us,
yet we feast upon the mercies of God,
who gives us the vision to move forward
against the shadows of what is unknown.
Our path is lit by the God we do know.

Question:

Can you trust God concerning the things in your life you don't see? . . . why, or why not?

NOTES/THOUGHTS:

Day 36

Hosea 6:6 **For I desired mercy, and not sacrifice; and the knowledge of God more than burnt offerings.**—(AV)

It is the mercy call that pulls us in,
and no ceremony can endure it.
Not knowing God we will leave the altar,
for the hands will fail if the heart is weak.
To return his love beyond enduring.

Question:

What to you is the core of what should be faith and hope?

NOTES/THOUGHTS:

Day 37

Isaiah 6:8 **Also I heard the voice of the Lord, saying,**
   Whom shall I send and who will go for us?
   Then said I, Here am I; send me.—(AV)

To each one he calls
is the choice to answer him.
Voices waited for.

Questions:

If God were to call you, are you willing to respond?

Do you think that God would call for the "perfect you"? . . .
or does he just want you for you?

NOTES/THOUGHTS:

Day 38

Isaiah 11:9 **They shall not hurt or destroy in all my holy mountain: for the earth shall be full of the knowledge of the Lord, as the waters cover the sea.**—(AV)

"I see a mountain!"
"I have a dream!"
A place, a promise, a point of no return.

Questions:

Can there really, ever be a place for the realization of all good things?

Can there be a place where all that is "bad" cannot enter in?

Should there be such a place?

NOTES/THOUGHTS:

Day 39

Isaiah 12:3 **Therefore with joy shall ye draw water out of the wells of salvation.**—(AV)

North of Mexico, south of Borrego,
a spring in the desert, in the badlands;
but for the creatures there it is their home,
the scrub growing around it, their shelter.
In Spring it is the glory of God's throne.

Question:

Is there a place you can go to that lifts you out of all your problems?

NOTES/THOUGHTS:

Day 40

Isaiah 40:3-5 **From the wild places comes a great cry,**
   "The Lord is coming, make way!
   An unbending highway in the desert will be made
   for God! Valleys will rise up to support it.
   Mountains will bow down to make it level.
   It will be uncurved and regular.
   It will reflect God's glory, which will be revealed.
   And there will be no mistaking it, for God has spoken
   it into being!"—(iffy)

There is something wonderful when God speaks.
It is not that he just says something;
but his words and his deeds are bound with purpose.
There is a reason, and every inch of his plan has eternal
value.
In the place God dwells . . . there are no castoffs.

Questions:

What could be the purpose of God's highway?

Why do you think it would come from the desert?

NOTES/THOUGHTS:

Day 41

Matthew 6:21 **For where your treasure is, there will your heart be also.**—(AV)

Questions:

What is the value of your heart?

Is it sold cheaply, or for a high price?

NOTES/THOUGHTS:

Day 42

Matthew 6:34 **Don't worry about tomorrow,
tomorrow will deal with its own trouble.
It is enough that today is well stocked with
problems.**—(iffy)

<u>Questions:</u>

Has your thoughts about "tomorrow" stopped you from thinking about the next minute? . . . or right "now"?

Can tomorrow paralyze your today?

NOTES/THOUGHTS:

Day 43

Matthew 7:7,8 **"If you ask, you will get it. If you seek, you will find it.**
If you knock on a door, it will be opened to you.
For the principle is: the one who asks, receives;
and the one who seeks, finds;
and the door will always be opened for the one who knocks."—(iffy)

Questions:

What is it that you want from God? . . . and why?

Perhaps you don't want anything at all . . . and why would that be?

NOTES/THOUGHTS:

Day 44

Matthew 7:12 **"What do you want from others?**
How do you want them to treat you?
Don't wait for them: you do what you want from
them—to them.
This is the fulfillment of God's word!"—(iffy)

Questions:

Have you been waiting a long time for something good to happen to you?

Could it be that whatever good things that are in other folks' lives, are in your life, too?

NOTES/THOUGHTS:

Day 45

Matthew 7:1,2 **"Would you pass sentence on somebody?**
It could unlock the gate for the same thing to happen to you, too.
The weight of your condemnation of another might find its home on your shoulders"—(iffy)

Doom falls to darkness,
dragging us with earthbound chains.
Love soars to heaven.

Questions:

What kind of stopgap decisions, whether good or not so good, have you made in your life?

Are they patchwork choices that might still be leaking at the seams?

NOTES/THOUGHTS:

Day 46

Matthew 8:2,3 **A man with leprosy kneeled before Jesus.**
"Master, you can heal me, if you want to!"
And Jesus reached out to the man and touched him; and he said, "I want to. Be clean."
At that moment the man was healed.—(iffy)

Questions:

What do you have to ask of Jesus?

What do you think he would want from you?

NOTES/THOUGHTS:

Day 47

Psalm 72:12 **For he [God] shall deliver the needy when he crieth; the poor also, and him that hath no helper.**—(AV)

The shroud we cover ourselves with to hide
from the tomorrows that loom in our minds.
"Go away! Go away!" and raise our hands,
warding off the cruelty of the unknown.
But time is in every hidingplace.

Questions:

Hiding is such lonely work; could blessing be missing you, too?

Is it possible that God delights in lost causes?

NOTES/THOUGHTS:

Day 48

Matthew 8:19,20 **A lawyer of religion approached Jesus and said,**
"Teacher, where ever you go, I will follow!"
But Jesus responded, "The foxes have holes and the birds have nests, too.
But the Son of Man has no place to lay his head."—(iffy)

It seems that Jesus is exposed to
all the cold, troubling elements of this world.
There are no mysteries in Jesus' life.
The holy is plainspoken and truthful, ever serving in love
and in action.

Questions:

Where is the place of rest for truth?

Can it rest with you?

NOTES/THOUGHTS:

Day 49

Matthew 10:32,33 **[Jesus said] Whosoever therefore shall confess me before men, him I will confess also before my Father which is in heaven.**
But whosoever shall deny me before men,
him will I also deny before my Father which is in heaven.—(AV)

Questions:

When you hesitate with inaction and fear, does it lead to disappointment? . . . while things go on as they always have?

What opens the doors in our lives? . . . What closes them?

NOTES/THOUGHTS:

Day 50

Matthew 10:34 **Think not that I come to send peace on earth:**
   I came not to send peace, but a sword.—(AV)

Questions:

What is the cause of conflict in your life? . . . Why is it there?

Is there a "sword" in your life? . . . Does it have a purpose?

NOTES/THOUGHTS:

Day 51

Matthew 10:38 **"Whoever does not take up my afflic-
tion and take the way I have taken is not entitled
to my life."**—(iffy)

Sorrow and pain are to be avoided
at all costs in our life's economy.
Yet do we lose something without the splash
and battering of real problems and troubles?
. . . our world unlocked by a season of pain?

Question:

Are you putting off "troubles" only to find new problems
replacing them?

NOTES/THOUGHTS:

Day 52

Matthew 10:39 **"Grasping one's life tightly, it filters between your fingers and is gone.**
But the one who lets it go finds life renewed!"—(iffy)

My life moves with time,
its patterns are meant to flow.
I will stop—nothing.

Question:

If what you value most you've hidden, what is the cost?

NOTES/THOUGHTS:

Day 53

Matthew 12:36,37 **"There is a value with words, even if they're wasted, that will ultimately have to be accounted for.**
And it will be your words that will either save you, or they will condemn you."—(iffy)

Questions:

Do you speak out of love? . . . or could you care less?

What if you had to swallow your words? . . . how would they taste?

NOTES/THOUGHTS:

Day 54

Mark 4:21,22 **And Jesus said, "A lamp is not lit to put in storage or under a bed, is it?**
Where is the place for light that it is to be seen?
One day all things will be seen, regardless of whether they've been a secret or if they've been hidden.
They will come before the light."—(iffy)

A beams rays alight
the path of the traveler.
Beauty of purpose.

Questions:

Do you think that the clarity of light could heal the deepest pain?

Could exposing your darkest moments to the light somehow lift your heart? . . . or would it crush you?

NOTES/THOUGHTS:

Day 55

Mark 6:46 **And, after he'd sent his followers away, Jesus climbed a mountain alone to pray.**—(iffy)

Questions:

Do you think that prayer is alone-time?

So many important things for Jesus to do . . . why break away in the middle of everything?

NOTES/THOUGHTS:

Day 56

Mark 8:11,12 **The very religious people argued with Jesus, they wanted him to perform a spiritual sign. Inwardly frustrated, he said, "Why do you look for signs?**
You, as a group, won't be allowed to receive them."—(iffy)

Question:

Have you placed any conditions or limits on God?

NOTES/THOUGHTS:

Day 57

Mark 10:15 **"I'm telling you the truth, whoever refuses to see God's kingdom as a child would, also refuses to enter into God's kingdom."**—(iffy)

Keys shaped certain
ways open particular doors . . .
others will stay closed.

<u>Question:</u>

Does life appear to be too complex for you?

NOTES/THOUGHTS:

Day 58

Mark 10:51,52 **And Jesus answered and said unto him,**
What wilt thou that I should do unto thee?
The blind man said unto him,
Lord, that I might receive my sight.
And Jesus said unto him, Go thy way: thy faith
hath made thee whole.
And immediately he received his sight,
and followed Jesus in the way.—(AV)

Questions:

Jesus said, " . . . thy faith hath made thee whole" . . . how
can **faith** accomplish anything?

Jesus said, "Go thy way"; the now-seeing blind man chose
to follow Jesus . . . why?

NOTES/THOUGHTS:

Day 59

Mark 11:25,26 **"Prayer is a place of forgiveness.
If you cannot forgive, God will not respond to you.
If you do not forgive, you will find yourself
outside of God's forgiveness, too.**"—(iffy)

What is it like for you on the outside
always having to look at the inside?
Is it a sense that you're missing something
that you just can't quite put your finger on?
The entrance is just around the corner.

Questions:

Are you missing something?

How are you trying to figure it out?

NOTES/THOUGHTS:

Day 60

Mark 12:10 **And have ye not read this scripture; The stone which the builders rejected is become the head of the corner?**—(AV)

<u>Questions:</u>

How has your life been built, so far?

Is there anything that you've missed?

NOTES/THOUGHTS:

Day 61

Luke 1:37 **"For with God nothing shall be
    impossible."**—(iffy)

It always seems, at least to me it does,
that our lives are filled with difficulties,
restrictions and impossibilities.
Yet there's this angel who speaks to our lives
that nothing is impossible with God.

Questions:

Can we relate to such a thing?

How could you relate to such a thing?

NOTES/THOUGHTS:

Day 62

Matthew 4:4 **"In the Bible it says, 'Food, by itself, does not keep a person alive.**
But the words from God's mouth give us life.'"—(iffy)

Questions:

What is in you that transcends your physical hunger?

What fills your heart?

NOTES/THOUGHTS:

Day 63

Matthew 5:3 **"The happiness of those who acknowledge their spiritual poverty, the kingdom of
heaven consists of them"**—(iffy)

Question:

How honest are you in your appraisal of where you are in
your life?

NOTES/THOUGHTS:

Day 64

Matthew 5:4 **"There is happiness through God who fills
the sorrowful vacuum of loss; his touch changes
things."**—(iffy)

If the wind blows through
a garden of fallen leaves . . .
God moves standing still.

Question:

What if one lets God into the saddest place?

What if you let God into your saddest place? . . . saddest
memory?

NOTES/THOUGHTS:

Day 65

Matthew 5:5 **"There is great happiness in the humble life; it will rule the earth."**—(iffy)

Mountains and sunlight!
Forests and waterfalls!
Broad deserts with blowing winds!
Tall clouds over the ocean!
And I am amazed!

Questions:

Do we master such things? . . . or does one tend to them?

NOTES/THOUGHTS:

Day 66

Matthew 5:6 **"There is happiness in the need to search for goodness; those who do will be filled."**—(iffy)

Questions:

What do we look for in one another?

What do you care to see in yourself?

NOTES/THOUGHTS:

Day 67

Matthew 5:7 **"There is happiness for those who practice and walk in mercy, for God will immerse them in mercy."**—(iffy)

Questions:

Where are you right now?

How did you get there?

NOTES/THOUGHTS:

Day 68

Matthew 5:8 **"There is great happiness for those with an open and sincere heart, they will have the purity of vision to see God."**—(iffy)

The shimmering of aspen in the wind
and granite mountains outstretched toward heaven,
rivers and oceans flowing and crashing.
They conceal and reveal the ways of God.
We look with the doubters, or with love.

Questions:

Is there happy laughter in your heart?

Have you ever had laughter in your heart?

NOTES/THOUGHTS:

Day 69

Matthew 5:9 **"Extremely happy are those who compose their lives and actions in peace, they are God's children."**—(iffy)

<u>Question:</u>

Is where you are who you are?

NOTES/THOUGHTS:

Day 70

Matthew 5:10 **"There is happiness for those who find themselves harassed for their commitment to doing 'the right thing', they are the citizens of the kingdom of God."**—(iffy)

Questions:

If you've encountered conflicts in your life, what was the problem?

What was your attitude?

NOTES/THOUGHTS:

Day 71

Psalm 34:8 **O taste and see that the Lord is good: blessed is the man that trusteth in him.**—(AV)

<u>Questions:</u>

An invitation, "try God" . . . can he be trusted? . . . is he worth a try?

NOTES/THOUGHTS:

Day 72

Matthew 6:24 **"Who can 'multi-task' under two superiors?**
You will always find yourself leaning toward one at the expense of the other; loyalty to one and betrayal of the other.
It's the same way with the pursuit of God and the pursuit of wealth: one or the other, but not both."—(iffy)

Questions:

Have you ever found yourself in a "conflict of interest" situation? . . . what was the cause?

NOTES/THOUGHTS:

Day 73

Matthew 7:13,14 **"There is a way to walk that is simple and straightforward.**
There is also the 'do it your own way' because 'you're in control!'
Most folks choose the 'do it your own way', and it leads to ruin.
But the way which is simple and straightforward guides us to life, and yet there are few that find it."—(iffy)

Questions:

Have you ever felt that you were in crowd but heading in the opposite direction of everyone else?

Isn't it easier to just "go with the flow"?

NOTES/THOUGHTS:

Day 74

Matthew 9:12,13 **"Who is strong? Do they need a
healer?**

**But it's those who are sick that need the touch of
one.**

Think about this saying [from God],

**'I'm looking for the life of compassion and not
for the empty formula of religion.'**

**If you see yourself as perfectly strong, then I
can't help you.**

**But for those who are 'heart-sick' and know
they are, I've come to draw their illness out of
them."**—(iffy)

Questions:

Where do you stand these days? . . . what does it feel
like?

NOTES/THOUGHTS:

Day 75

Psalm 22:24 **For he [God] won't look down on, nor shrink from those suffering; and he won't turn his back on them either.**
He does just the opposite of that.
God listens for the cry of the afflicted.—(iffy)

Questions:

Have you cried?

Why would God be interested in your tears?

NOTES/THOUGHTS:

Day 76

Psalm 37:16 **The poverty of a good and honorable person is riches and the wealth of the many who are bad and unprincipled is like an empty coin purse.**—(iffy)

The stock market crashed,
yet there is love in my heart.
What passes? What stays?

Questions:

What is the greatest treasure in your heart?

Can it be purchased?

NOTES/THOUGHTS:

Day 77

Psalm 36:9 **For with thee is the fountain of life: in thy light shall we see light.**—(AV)

<u>Question:</u>

What can you, can I, possibly do to "see light" in the way this verse says?

NOTES/THOUGHTS:

Day 78

Daniel 3:16-18 " **. . . we are not terribly concerned about your response to our answer, oh king.**
We serve our God, and he is able to frustrate your desire to punish us by burning us alive.
Yet, even if he doesn't save us from the fire, you need to understand, sir, that we would still serve no other god!
And we will certainly not worship your man made golden idol!"—(iffy)

Questions:

Why would someone be willing to risk even fire to state their objections?

Have you ever been made to do something that you didn't feel good about? . . . how'd it feel?

NOTES/THOUGHTS:

Day 79

Philippians 4:7 **God's peace, which is totally beyond our comprehension, will put you at rest in Christ Jesus, and your minds will be protected!**—(iffy)

Mostly people say
they get by in any way.
But is it enough?

Questions:

Is your heart troubled?

What would it mean to you to have complete peace of mind?

NOTES/THOUGHTS:

Day 80

Philippians 4:8 **Finally, brethren, whatsoever things are true, whatsoever things are honest, whatsoever things are just, whatsoever things are pure, whatsoever things are lovely, whatsoever things are of good report; if there be any virtue, and if there be any praise, think on these things.**—(AV)

Questions:

Could you picture, in your mind, reaching for something "wonderful"?

In your heart . . . what are you reaching for?

NOTES/THOUGHTS:

Day 81

Philippians 4:13 **I can do all things through Christ which strengtheneth me.**—(AV)

Questions:

Have you hit a wall in your life?

What would you do with yourself if you able to overcome all of your obstacles? . . . your problems?

NOTES/THOUGHTS:

Day 82

Colossians 1:17 **Before all things were, Christ is.**
He is the ultimate rule which holds all things
together.—(iffy)

I climb the long climb
to where lines intersect,
the point of light—Christ.

Questions:

How are you holding together right now?

If you're having difficulty . . . do you think that Christ could
help? . . . why, or why not?

NOTES/THOUGHTS:

Day 83

Job 9:15 **"What if I were right and good and innocent,
   but had nothing to prove it so?
   I would ask of God to judge me."**—(iffy)

If I am alone in my own regard
and cannot be heard, but rather ignored,
perhaps I will doubt my own innocence
without an honest voice to comfort me.
A voice! And it doesn't have to agree.

Questions:

Where is our life's validation?

Does it come by itself?

NOTES/THOUGHTS:

Day 84

Job 10:8 **"You [God] have made me, inside and out. Yet you undo me."**—(iffy)

Questions:

Is God really ever done with us? . . . or do you wonder if God is involved with us at all?

NOTES/THOUGHTS:

Day 85

Psalm 127:1 **If the blueprints aren't drawn from God, the builder will find his project an excercise in futility.**
A city is always imperiled if God is excluded from its counsels.—(iffy)

Nests blown down by winds,
yet birds persist in building.
Come spring eggs will hatch.

Questions:

How have you started in your life?

How do you want to finish?

NOTES/THOUGHTS:

Day 86

Genesis 12:1 **God called Abram, in his circumstances,
and told him, "Leave your country and your family,
walk away from the household of your father.
I will show you the land where you are to go."**—(iffy)

A future that holds unseen potential
and yet the future lurks in the shadows
that is simply elemental of time.
You cannot reshape to you own desire
the choice taken, but to move boldly on.

Questions:

If God invites you, would you go?

What do you think is the difference between faith and
uncertainty?

NOTES/THOUGHTS:

Day 87

Genesis 16:13 **She called God by his name, "You, God, see me!" because he spoke to her as she prayed. She pondered, "I live, even as I've seen him."**—(iffy)

The sacred moments
are places of great peril.
The truth sears my heart.

Questions:

How accessible do you think God is to you?

Do you want to be able to see God?

NOTES/THOUGHTS:

Day 88

Genesis 28:16,17 **Jacob woke up and said, "God is here and I didn't know it!"**
So he was afraid, then he said, "This is a place of dread!
This is where God's house is!
This is the gate of heaven!"—(iffy)

Jacob had a dream
that changed him in a moment.
For God sought him out.

Question:

Is God seeking you out?

NOTES/THOUGHTS:

Day 89

Genesis 50:19,20 **Joseph responded to his brothers,**
   "Don't be afraid of me. Would I presume to act
   as God?
   Still, you planned to do evil against me.
   Yet God's intention, through all this, was good;
   accomplishing the saving of all our lives.
   Here we are, all of us, right now!"—(iffy)

Question:

If you look back at yesterday can you see tomorrow?

NOTES/THOUGHTS:

Day 90

Exodus 23:2,3 **"You are not to do wrong and to cause harm just because 'almost everyone is doing it'.**
You are not to speak an 'untruth' so you can please public opinion when public opinion finds itself opposed to justice.
Nor do you overthrow justice in favor of the impoverished."—(iffy)

Question:

Wouldn't you feel bad if someone changed the rules and didn't tell you about it?

NOTES/THOUGHTS:

Day 91

Numbers 23:19 **"God is not human and so will not lie.**
He is not given to the mistakes of man that he
should regret them.
Does God waste his speech?
Has he ever said something that wasn't followed
up by him doing it?"—(iffy)

Question:

Do you want at least one thing that is dependable in your
life?

NOTES/THOUGHTS:

Day 92

Deuteronomy 16:20 **"What is openhearted, impartial and truthful?**
Well, that is the path to follow, to live in and to receive from; the path to the homeland that God gives you."—(iffy)

Question:

Could it be that the greatest place to live in this planet is on the road to God?

NOTES/THOUGHTS

Day 93

Job 21:22 **Shall any teach God knowledge?**
   See he judgeth those that are high.—(AV)

Questions:

Do you have resentment in your life? . . . are you frustrated?

If you are either, or both, what is at the core of these things in your life?

NOTES/THOUGHTS:

Day 94

Psalm 3:1,2 **Lord, how they are increased that trouble me!**
Many are they that rise up against me.
Many there be which say of my soul,
There is no help for him in God.—(AV)

Questions:

Have you found that the seed of criticism in your life has grown to outright hostility?

Is it fair to characterize God as someone who wouldn't help you?

NOTES/THOUGHTS:

Day 95

Psalm 5:7 **I am choosing to walk into the place of limitless mercy,**
I choose to walk into your house, Lord.
Your temple is where I'll bow down in humble worship.—(iffy)

Questions:

Is it an "honor" to worship God? . . . why, or why not?

NOTES/THOUGHTS:

Day 96

Psalm 9:18 **Those in need will not be left in limbo, and the afflicted will not go hopeless.**—(iffy)

It's a lonely world,
lives falling like leaves from trees.
Futile reflections.

<u>Question:</u>

Have you ever felt that help was unavailable to you?

NOTES/THOUGHTS:

Day 97

Psalm 18:1,2 **I will love you, God! You have empowered me!**

God has been my anchor, he has been my protector, he's been my resuer.

He's is my God and my rock.

I find sanctuary in him.

He intercedes for my safety and provides me with a strong shelter.—(iffy)

Question:

How would your daily life be altered if you walked with a sense of empowerment and of safety?

NOTES/THOUGHTS:

Day 98

Psalm 23:6 **Surely goodness and mercy shall follow me all the days of my life: and I will dwell in the house of the Lord forever.**—(AV)

Questions:

Wouldn't it be nice to hang onto those moments of serenity?

Have you ever had one of those moments?

NOTES/THOUGHTS:

Day 99

Psalm 27:4 **If there' one thing I've wanted from God, it's the one thing that I've always desired: I want to spend my life in the Lord's house, to just be in the wonder of his Presence and to be able to seek out his answers in his temple.**—(iffy)

Questions:

Has there ever been in your life someone or something that you just wanted to be close to? . . . just be in even close proximity to?

NOTES/THOUGHTS:

Day 100

Psalm 35:17,18 **God, are you just going to standby, looking on?**
These people are chewing up my soul and I need rescue!
They're like hungry lions who wont stop until I'm eaten up.
But, still, I will thank you in advance where your believers gather together.
And I will praise you for who you are before everyone!—(iffy)

Questions:

Have you been in a place that this verse describes?

Can faith overcome even before overcoming has happened?

NOTES/THOUGHTS:

Day 101

Psalm 36:7 **Lord, your love is the most important thing in my life.**
In the shelter of your wings all humanity can take refuge.—(iffy)

<u>Questions:</u>

What do you think of when you hear the word "shelter"?

What would you like it to mean for you?

NOTES/THOUGHTS:

Day 102

Psalm 39:4,5 **Lord, help me to understand the purpose at the end of my time and all that is truly me between "now" and "then", that I might be able to perceive my limitations.**
My time is, as it is, short and insignificant before you.
I know that every man and woman is really of a humble status in your presence.—(iffy)

Question:

What do you think it means to "know one's self"?

NOTES/THOUGHTS:

Day 103

Psalm 41:4 **Lord, extend yourself compassionately to me!**
I have hurt myself through fighting you
And now I need you to heal me.—(iffy)

<u>Question:</u>

Can there be a more humble request?

NOTES/THOUGHTS:

Day 104

Psalm 42:2 **My soul thirsteth for God, for the living God: when shall I come and appear before God?**—(AV)

Questions:

Is there an urgent desire in your life to settle everything right now, to just get it done with? . . . why, or why not?

NOTES/THOUGHTS:

Day 105

Psalm 42:5 **Why is my very being so depressed?**
   Why is there such a roar of anxiety within me?
   **I need to pull my attention from these things and
   insert my hope for God!**
   **Even now his attention to me is changing things;
   so how can I not praise him?**—(iffy)

The shadow of death
recedes before the sunlight.
. . . We're on the borders.

Questions:

Have you felt frustrated and empowered at the same time?

Have you had a sense of hope even in your most defeated
moments?

NOTES/THOUGHTS:

Day 106

Psalm 45:1 **Something good is bubbling over in my heart!**
I am composing it even as I speak; and it is transforming itself into a song of the King!—(iffy)

Questions:

Ecstasy in its spiritual form, I suppose?

Care to try?

NOTES/THOUGHTS:

Day 107

Psalm 46:1 **God is our refuge and strength, a very present help in trouble.**—(AV)

Questions:

How is it that some believe that God can help, while others don't?

How do you perceive God's capability and proximity?

NOTES/THOUGHTS:

Day 108

Psalm 46:4-6 **There, a river delighting God's city,**
    holy dwelling places of the Most High.
    She will not be moved for God is with her.
    In the morning he comes with great power,
    the world at odds he unseats with his
    voice!—(iffy)

Questions:

Can any place be free of trouble?

Can there ultimately be an end to trouble?

NOTES/THOUGHTS:

Day 109

Psalm 51:10 **I need the cleansing of my broken heart, Lord, and a transformation of my innermost being.**—(iffy)

Question:

Could it be that the worst place a person has ever been (you, for instance) is just the mid-point on an incredible journey?

NOTES/THOUGHTS:

Day 110

Psalm 51:16,17 **Lord, you don't want my religion (I can be religious, you know), rituals appear to be as nothing to you.**
But when I was reduced to humiliation; when my heart was crushed and bleeding before you, you looked at me.—(iffy)

Question:

Why must (at least some) people come to such a place before God comes to them?

NOTES/THOUGHTS:

Day 111

Psalm 55:4-8 **My heart is filled with tremendous anguish, and death terrors have fallen upon me. I shake with fear and tremble in horror.**
If I had wings like a dove
I could fly away and rest somewhere.
Think about it: I could wander off and always remain in the wilderness, escaping the windstorms and the cyclones.—(iffy)

Question:

It's so easy to want to flee into solitude when trouble is at its worst . . . but if you could . . . would you come back?

NOTES/THOUGHTS:

Day 112

Psalm 57:1 **Be merciful to me, God, be merciful to me!**
   For my whole being is trusting in you
   And I am taking refuge in the shadow of your
   wings until the storms of destruction have passed
   overhead. —(iffy)

Questions:

Why do some people choose to go it alone through the troubles in their lives?

Why are there the "needy"?

Where are you in the scheme of things?

NOTES/THOUGHTS:

Day 113

Psalm 55:22 **What are the deep burdens of your heart?**
Give them to God. He will hold you together.
Those who stand in him won't have reason to even quiver.—(iffy)

Questions:

Have you ever had deep disappointment in your life?

Do you feel that God has disappointed you? Why, or why not?

NOTES/THOUGHTS:

Day 114

Psalm 60:4,5 **There is a banner over those who worship you [Lord], it is there as a signal of truth to those who would seek truth.**
Those who come will be delivered and with your strength you will answer!—(iffy)

Questions:

Have you ever had identity problems?

What, or whom do you choose to identify with?

Or . . . do you choose nothing entirely?

NOTES/THOUGHTS:

Day 115

Psalm 61:1,2 **Hear my cry, O God; attend to my prayer.**
From the end of the earth will I cry unto thee, when my heart is overwhelmed: lead to the rock that is higher than I.—(AV)

Questions:

Have you ever wanted to be "above it all"?

Why? . . . and was it for the right reasons, do you think?

NOTES/THOUGHTS:

Day 116

Psalm 62:5-8 **My soul wait quietly for God alone,**
for the only hope I have is from him.
God, my foundation and my salvation, the fortress
from which I won't be moved.
On the saving God let my praises rest;
safety in he who is the foundation of strength.
People's trust should be in him, always.
We can trust him with all that's in our hearts,
because he is the God of refuge for all of us!—(iffy)

Questions:

Where do you place your trust?

Is that "place" worthy?

NOTES/THOUGHTS:

Day 117

Psalm 63:1,2 **God, in all things I will acknowledge you.**
I live in a place that is like a barren desert in need of your living waters, and I thirst for you.
Because of my desire I have seen you in the place of my prayers.
I have beheld your power and the wonder of your presence.—(iffy)

Questions:

Are you in a place where you can acknowledge anything? . . . and if so, what?

Where would you like to be?

NOTES/THOUGHTS:

Day 118

Psalm 68:5,6 **He is the father to those who are orphaned.**
He is the advocate for the widowed.
This is the Lord in his dwelling place, where he opens his doors to the lonely.
He returns to the condemned a full life.
Only those who disagree with true love and mercy will find themselves in the dry land.—(iffy)

Question:

Are you alone in the middle of nowhere?

NOTES/THOUGHTS:

Day 119

Psalm 69:5 **God you know my foolish behavior and you haven't been fooled by mistakes.**—(iffy)

Questions:

Isn't it uncomfortable when you are totally exposed, from the inside, out?

Who would accept you?

But do you always want to hide?

NOTES/THOUGHTS:

Day 120

Psalm 69:32,33 **The humble have witnessed this joyously!
And let those who follow God be refreshed in their hearts!
For the Lord responds to the needy and he stands with those in captivity!**—(iffy)

Humble is the place
where we see God move in lives.
We behold ourselves.

Question:

Who can identify with you when you feel that you're excluded from everything?

NOTES/THOUGHTS:

Day 121

Psalm 71:9 **Cast me not off in the time of my old age;
forsake me not when my strength faileth.**—(AV)

When we come to the realization
that we won't be as we are, right now,
the so-called "control of our destiny"
becomes silly, banal and laughable
as we hobble into reality.

Question:

What do you have set aside for when your soul retires?

NOTES/THOUGHTS:

Day 122

Psalm 72:13,14 **He will reach out to those reduced to begging and in dire need.**
And he will be able to save even the weakest.
He will lift them from the web of lies and physical intimidation.
He will count every ounce of their lives as most precious; their blood his blood.—(iffy)

Our pain, a treasure,
a cause for transformation.
What's dearest to God?

Questions:

But what about the internal conflicts; the battles one wakes up to?

What does one do with a bleeding heart?

NOTES/THOUGHTS:

Day 123

Psalm 73:21-24 **My whole being was filled with bitterness, as if I'd been stabbed in the back. Consequently, I acted stupidly, paranoid, like a mad bull in your presence [O God]. But even so, I'm not going to leave you. You calmly took my life into your hands. You walked me out and above that attitude of anger, to the place of radiant honor.**—(iffy)

Questions:

Are our lives designed to exist in the thoughts of our worst fears and expectations?

Is the bitterness in our lives there because of what has happened to us? . . .

Or is it there because of what we've allowed events to do to our attitude?

NOTES/THOUGHTS:

Day 124

Psalm 73:25,26 **My confession is you, Lord, and only you before all heaven.**
I will walk on the face of the earth, but I will walk after you.
I walk in a body with its limitations; yet, even so, I find myself without limitations with God's strength in my life, forever.—(iffy)

Question:

Could it be that true power, in our lives, is something beyond our comprehension?

NOTES/THOUGHTS:

Day 125

Psalm 76:2,3 **God's pavillion is in Peace which is his Fortress, where he dwells: here are extinguished all the tools of devastation and war.**—(iffy)

A kindly moment,
cool winds blowing from sunrise.
My heart a temple.

Question:

Is there such a sacred place in your heart?

NOTES/THOUGHTS:

Day 126

Psalm 84:3,4 **The smallest finches are at home with you [God], and the mother swallow raises her young at his alters, in the presence of the Lord of Hosts. There is great praise for you, God; for all of those who live with you are filled with blessings.**—(iffy)

Questions:

Is the thought of holiness a place of fearfulness for you?

Or is it a nurturing home?

NOTES/THOUGHTS:

Day 127

Psalm 85:10-13 **Mercy and truth are met together;
righteousness and peace have kissed eachother.
Truth shall spring out of the earth;
and righteousness shall look down from heaven.
Yea, the Lord shall give that which is good;
and our land shall yield her increase.
Righteousness shall go before him; and shall set
us in the way of his steps.**—(AV)

Questions:

Is prosperity in the things that we have? . . .

. . . Or is prosperity derived from a place in the heart?

NOTES/THOUGHTS:

Day 128

Psalm 86:1-3 **O Lord, hear me! For I have nothing and I need you.**

I have bound myself to you and only you can preserve me.

So, God, will you save me?

Because my holiness is in my dependence upon you.

O Lord, I need your touch of mercy every day; and every day I am before you!—(iffy)

Question:

If God were to have an economy, would there be room there for the self-made man or the self-made woman?

NOTES/THOUGHTS:

Day 129

Psalm 88:1,4 **You are my saving God, O Lord!**
There are no hours in my day when I have not
cried to you.
In this world I am merely one waiting for death:
I am literally crushed by such callousness.—(iffy)

Question:

Are you a statistic?

NOTES/THOUGHTS:

Day 130

Psalm 92:1,2 **It is a good thing to give thanks unto the Lord, and to sing praises unto thy name, O most High:**
To show forth in the morning, and thy faithfulness every night,—(AV)

Questions:

Is your life full?

And, even if it appears to be, do you still have a sense of emptiness?

NOTES/THOUGHTS:

Day 131

Psalm 97:11,12 **God has embedded light and joy in the hearts of those who stand in him and are filled with his love.**
A cause for celebrating the Lord, his name more than worthy of our thanks.—(iffy)

Light and joy, the place of celebration.
Beyond the dreams of those folded in pain,
standing apart from the invitation.
Yet it still stands, beckoning them to come,
to illumination and to gladness.

Question:

If there is a party and you're invited, why wouldn't you come?

NOTES/THOUGHTS:

Day 132

Psalm 100:5 **All that is God is good.**
   His mercy is eternal mercy.
   His truth never changes; he endures for all lives
   to come.—(iffy)

Questions:

Does something constant mean boredom to you?

However, would you like at least one thing that is dependable in your life?

NOTES/THOUGHTS:

Day 133

Psalm 102:25-28 **The beginning for us was when you fashioned the earth and with your hands formed heaven.**
And they will ultimately pass away, the energy of their movement will wear them out.
Yet even they will be renewed by you!
But you [Lord] are and will always be!
All who are yours will continue with you!—(iffy)

Question:

When everything around us seems and feels so bleak . . . where will you find a hope worth hanging onto?

NOTES/THOUGHTS:

Day 134

Psalm 103:8-12 **The Lord is filled with love and forgiveness.**
**It takes a lot to provoke him, but he's ever so quick
to extend his compassion.**
**He will say what the problem is, but he will not hold
a grudge.**
**We've done wrong, yet he restrains himself; his
love versus our iniquity.**
**It is like the span from where we stand going up to
the stars and that broad expanse is filled with his
love for us who call on him.**
**Look to where the sun rises and then look to where
the sun sets: he has thrown from us our guilt, from
horizon to horizon.**—(iffy)

Questions:

What is the limit of your patience?

Have you been pushed so far that there is no room in your
life for mercy?

NOTES/THOUGHTS:

THE TRAVELS AND TREVAILS OF PSALM 107
(The Pilgrims' Journey)

Day 135

Psalm 107:1-3 **There's every reason to thank God: he is good forever; his love is forever, too!**
He went so far as to rescue us from deep, deep trouble.
We should, in return, share his love.
The love of the Lord who has drawn us all to him, from every corner of the world.—(iffy)

Questions:

Is your life filled with excuses?

If it is, are your excuses merely putting of what is eventual?

NOTES/THOUGHTS:

Day 136

Psalm 107:4 **Before we came to the Lord we were lost in a lonely desert without any hint of town or shelter.**—(iffy)

Questions:

Have you ever found that even in the fun moments of your life there's still a little bit of nagging emptiness?

If you have, did you find that emptiness opening into a wider expanse as you "went along"?

NOTES/THOUGHTS:

Day 137

Psalm 107:5 **Before we came to the Lord we were hungry and thirsty, ready to die, inside and out.**—(iffy)

Question:

Have you ever felt, sometimes, that even your highest aspirations seem disappointing to your deepest hopes?

NOTES/THOUGHTS:

Day 138

Psalm 107:6 **Then, right in the middle of everything, we pleaded to the Lord and he rescued us.**—(iffy)

Question:

Could it be that the answers to our problem, our quanderies, are just a request away?

NOTES/THOUGHTS:

Day 139

Psalm 107:7 **The path of our rescue leads straight to a city of life.**—(iffy)

Question:

Wouldn't it be nice if truth had a direct payoff?

NOTES/THOUGHTS:

Day 140

Psalm 107:8 **Thankfulness should be given to the Lord, because he confirms his goodness through action.**—(iffy)

Known lonely places
comforted by God's presence.
Light scatters darkness.

Questions:

Is your biggest need a change of circumstance?

Or is your biggest need a change of heart?

NOTES/THOUGHTS:

Day 141

Psalm 107:9 **For the soul that yearns unknowingly, he satisfies.**
The soul that has been empty, he fills with goodness.—(iffy)

Question:

Is your heart dark simply because it's empty?

NOTES/THOUGHTS:

Day 142

Psalm 107:10-14 **They cling to darkness, those who have confined themselves to the curtains of death.**
Chained by their refusal to hear what God had to say, thinking that the Lord's wisdom was beneath them.
So he left them with no answers for their empty hearts.
And they found themselves abandoned and alone. That's when they prayed to the Lord, in their trouble; and out of their trouble he saved them. All the traps and chains of darkness and death were smashed, and the Lord brought them out to the light!—(iffy)

Question:

Have you ever taken something on in your life and half-way through realized that you'd bitten off more than you could chew?

NOTES/THOUGHTS:

Day 143

Psalm 107:15,16 **Wouldn't it be good for people to praise God?**
For true praise is for the real things that he has done for us; the walls imprisoning our souls, he shattered!—(iffy)

Question:

Have you ever kept quiet when you really should have said something?

NOTES/THOUGHTS:

Day 144

Psalm 107:17-20 **People made themselves foolish because they said "no" to God, their lives bent to do wrong, they inflicted wrong upon themselves. They restricted their diet, as if that would save them, but it only led them to death's door.**
Then they panicked and cried to the Lord and he saved them.
He corrected their paths and led them from their self-destruction.—(iffy)

I took a boat with a friend and a lover.
I was going to pull it upstream with wine.
In my strength I would challenge the current which wore me down and I let go of them.
What strength I had left I clung to a rock.

Question:

Can you get on with your life all by yourself?

NOTES/THOUGHTS:

Day 145

Psalm 107:21,22 **So wouldn't it be good for people to praise God?**
He came through and saved people in need; so shouldn't they say something about it with a spirit of thanksgiving?—(iffy)

Questions:

Shouldn't they? . . . Shouldn't we?

NOTES/THOUGHTS:

Day 146

Psalm 107:23-30 **The seafarers have seen the Lord move and his glory rise from the ocean.**
The winds rise at his word and the waves mount up to meet them, only to crash down into the valleys of the deep.
And the seafarers are afflicted between the waters and the sky; helpless they cry to God.
And God has saved them.
The waves cease, yet he constrains the winds to gently guide the seafarers to a safe harbor.
They are more than thankful.—(iffy)

Questions:

Could this have been an anecdote that the psalmist is relaying, a life experience?

What have been your life experiences concerning perils?

NOTES/THOUGHTS:

Day 147

107:31,32 **Again I'd like to say, wouldn't it be good for people to praise God?**
Shouldn't people, shouldn't every segment of society, be made aware that God is?
That God responds to us and saves us?

Questions:

Is there a covert need for "thanksgiving" in your life?

What would happen to your innermost person if you just let go and thanked God?

NOTES/THOUGHTS:

Day 148

Psalm 107:33-37 **Flowing rivers and bubbling springs are turned into a dry parched desert by God.**
The wickedness of people destroys their own fruitful land.
Yet God turns a barren place into a land of lakes and streams; where those who've been starving **are given food and shelter.**
They build a community and harvest from the land.—(iffy)

Question:

Do you squander your opportunities and yet ask for more?

NOTES/THOUGHTS:

Day 149

Psalm 107:38,39 **God touches with blessing those who had misfortune; his purpose is to increase their blessing.**
But oppression, hurt and pain come from another direction, and they come to obliterate joy and blessing.—(iffy)

Questions:

Are you caught "in between"?

Do you have choices to make?

NOTES/THOUGHTS:

Day 150

Psalm 107:40-43 **But God despises oppression and places those that do it into their own desert place; they're trapped by their own desires.**
Those who were victims become God's family.
Joy for those who make their stand in God.
Evil will become defenseless.
If any person is considerate and smart and observant they will, without a doubt, see God's love in action!—(iffy)

Questions:

Where is "love" in your life?

Is "love" convenient sometimes . . . all the time . . . or rarely?

NOTES/THOUGHTS:

Day 151

Psalm 35:1 **Lord, I'm asking you to stand between those who are my enemies and me; push back on those who have been pushing me around.**—(iffy)

The problem with failure is that we think
we must succeed, and succeed on our own.
But success and failure are small factors.
They are things we walk through in a full
life as we follow Christ, by faith, in his love.

Questions:

Do you feel like you struggle alone?

Are you tired?

NOTES/THOUGHTS:

Day 152

John 1:29 **On the very next day, John [the Baptist]
watched Jesus approach him.
And, as Jesus was still walking toward him, John
said,
"Look! Here is the Lamb of God!
All the corruption of the world will be removed
by him!"**—(iffy)

Question:

How can a LAMB right wrongs and take away evil?

NOTES/THOUGHTS:

Day 153

Matthew 10:30 **But the very hairs of your head are all numbered.**—(AV)

Question:

Why do you think God would pay so much attention, if he does?

NOTES/THOUGHTS:

Day 154

1 Corinthians 16:13 **The mature adult is strong; and in this manner that is where you are to stand in faith.**—(iffy)

<u>Questions:</u>

Are you looking for your place in the sun?

Do you think you've found it but someone else is already standing there?

NOTES/THOUGHTS:

Day 155

Philippians 2:5-7 **You should be thinking this way, this is the way Jesus thought: his life is the life of God, he was content in himself to be God, but he stepped out of that and into the human life, an unknown servant.**
(As he thought, so he did.)—(iffy)

Question:

Is it important to be important?

NOTES/THOUGHTS:

Day 156

Psalm 23:4 **Yea, though I walk through the valley of
the shadow of death,
I will fear no evil: for thou art with me, thy rod
and thy staff they comfort me.**—(AV)

Question:

What is the problem with depression for you?

NOTES/THOUGHTS:

Day 157

Psalm 115:3 **But our God is in the heavens: he hath done whatsoever he hath pleased.**—(AV)

Question:

If God isn't fixed in stone, or on an altar, or on the wall; how does one relate to him?

NOTES/THOUGHTS:

Day 158

Psalm 116:1-4 **My love for the Lord comes from experiencing him answering my prayers.**
He listened to me, he heard me!
My whole life will be a prayer to him.
My life was a life of mourning.
I was sunk in the deepest valley of despair and depression.
The harder I looked to get out, the more problems and sadness seemed to grow.
But then I called out for the Lord,
"Lord! I'm pleading for my life here!"—(iffy)

Questions:

Do you feel that your heart, your mind, your very being are in peril?

Is there a place in your heart that you can go to that will help you to feel a little more secure?

NOTES/THOUGHTS:

Day 159

Psalm 118:22 **The stone which the builders refused is become the headstone of the corner.**—(AV)

It's in this way that Christ is discarded
by people whose perception was clouded.
He just didn't fit the popular mold.

Question?:

Do you feel that others try to shape your life into what they imagine for you?

How do you feel about that?

How should you respond (if that is true)?

NOTES/THOUGHTS:

Day 160

Psalm 121:5-8 **The preserving Lord defends and works through your life.**
He holds the sun and the moon in their place.
The Lord takes his stand against evil, preserving your life.
As you come and go God defends you.
He's not committed to you for a moment; but for eternity.—(iffy)

Questions:

What are your concerns?

What are your needs?

Can you conclusively resolve them, or do you need help?

NOTES/THOUGHTS:

Day 161

Psalm 126:6 **The burdened heart, filled with purpose, and yet disappointed will doubtless come back in full circle with joy and fulfillment!**—(iffy)

<u>Question:</u>

Can you move forward in your life, sight unseen, and yet still persevere in hope?

NOTES/THOUGHTS:

Day 162

Psalm 130:3,4 **Lord, none of us could stand for one minute if you were inclined to punish us for our errors.**
On the contrary, respect for you is due for your heart of forgiveness.—(iffy)

Questions:

The imperfection of humankind . . . is it so universal?

The nature of God . . . can his forgiveness be so worthy?

NOTES/THOUGHTS:

Day 163

Psalm 136:1 **Thank the Lord! The quality of his goodnes and love goes on forever.**—(iffy)

Question:

What is the limit of your endurance?

NOTES/THOUGHTS:

Day 164

Psalm 136:2 **Thank the Lord! The basis of his rulership is his enduring love.**—(iffy)

Question:

Do you see "power" as some thing that originates from a source other than love?

NOTES/THOUGHTS:

Day 165

Psalm 136:3 **Thank the Lord! His hold on power is his enduring love.**—(iffy)

Question:

Is your "strength" based upon something other than love?

NOTES/THOUGHTS:

Day 166

Psalm 136:4 **Give thanks to God! Because he takes action and he intervenes on account of his love.**—(iffy)

Question:

When you do something for somebody, what is at the core of your motivation?

NOTES/THOUGHTS:

Day 167

Psalm 136:5 **At the heart of this universe is God's love.**—(iffy)

Question:

Could you align yourself with this thought, or not?

NOTES/THOUGHTS:

Day 168

Psalm 136:6 **Thank the Lord! For the blueprint of our environment is embued with his love.**—(iffy)

Question:

If this has occurred to you, have you ever wondered why certain nature scenes tug at your insides with yearning?

NOTES/THOUGHTS:

Day 169

Psalm 136:7 **Thank the Lord! For in the stars and in the dawning of the day we see reflections of his love.**—(iffy)

Questions:

Is God's love disguised?

Or is God's love more apparent than we think?

NOTES/THOUGHTS:

Day 170

Psalm 136:8 **Thank the Lord! The greatness and purpose of the sun are because of his love.**—(iffy)

Question:

Could God's love be immeasurably greater than anything that we could possibly perceive?

NOTES/THOUGHTS:

Day 171

Psalm 136:9 **Thank the Lord! The reflections and evening signs are moving emblems of his love.**—(iffy)

Question:

If these things are really extensions of God's love; can the variations of those patterns and designs be calculated?

NOTES/THOUGHTS:

Day 172

Psalm 136:10 **Thank the Lord! Even in the hard hand of punishment we see the implacability of his love.**—(iffy)

Questions:

Is "the moment of truth" an end? . . . or is it merely a beginning?

NOTES/THOUGHTS:

Day 173

Psalm 136:11 **Thank the Lord! For the character of his deliverance is dictated by his love.**—(iffy)

<u>Questions:</u>

What is salvation?

What is the nature of the Person behind salvation?

NOTES/THOUGHTS:

Day 174

Psalm 136:12 **Thank the Lord! For the strength of his leading is in the hands of his love.**—(iffy)

Question:

Can one truly follow "to the end" that which is hated and hateful?

NOTES/THOUGHTS:

Day 175

Psalm 136:13 **Thank the Lord! For the greatness and the exercise of his power is founded upon his love.**—(iffy)

Questions:

What, or whom, do you feel is worthy of your trust?

Have you ever been betrayed?

NOTES/THOUGHTS:

Day 176

Psalm 136:14 **Thank the Lord! For he not only acts on behalf of his people, but he moves and walks with them because of his love.**—(iffy)

Question:

The God who is a participator in your life; can you handle that?

NOTES/THOUGHTS:

Day 177

Psalm 136:15 **Thank the Lord! For destruction falls upon those who refuse to see and obey his love.**—(iffy)

Questions:

Is there a flipside to complete love?

Or is it that there are simply repercussions to the absence of love?

NOTES/THOUGHTS:

Day 178

Psalm 136:16 **Thank the Lord! Because we find that in the hard places endurance comes through his love.**—(iffy)

Question:

Is it possible that love can empower us beyond our expectations and comprehension?

NOTES/THOUGHTS:

Day 179

Psalm 136:17 **Thank the Lord! History is established, ebbs and flows, at the insistence of his love.**—(iffy)

Question:

When you look at history, or even at your own personal history, do you feel that there is something missing?

NOTES/THOUGHTS:

Day 180

Psalm 136:18 **Thank the Lord! For however great, one must acquiesce or fail before the purpose in his love.**—(iffy)

Questions:

What kind of "lines are drawn" in the world today?

Could they be reduced to simply LOVE on this side and APATHY on the other?

NOTES/THOUGHTS:

Day 181

Psalm 136:19 **Thank the Lord! Even the great and the bold must bow or be destroyed, for God's love is relentless.**—(iffy)

<u>Question:</u>

Can you derive comfort from the possibility that ultimate accountability must arrive at love's door?

NOTES/THOUGHTS:

Day 182

Psalm 136:20 **Thank the Lord! For even the most prominent and celebrated will not be: they will disappear, if they do not align themselves with his love.**—(iffy)

Questions:

Do you want fifteen minutes of fame? . . . or do you want something else?

NOTES/THOUGHTS:

Day 183

Psalm 136:21 **Thank the Lord! For possessions are scattered if they are not subordinated to the purposes of his love.**—(iffy)

<u>Questions:</u>

What do you have? . . . What do you hold in your hand?

Are they the sum total of who you are?

NOTES/THOUGHTS:

Day 184

Psalm 136:22 **Thank the Lord! He keeps his promises and he provides for his people because of his love.**—(iffy)

Question:

Have you ever experienced enduring and constant love?

NOTES/THOUGHTS:

Day 185

Psalm 136:23 **Thank the Lord! He does not forget us, nor neglect us, because that is not the character of his love.**—(iffy)

<u>Questions:</u>

In the scheme of things . . . where do you think you are?

Where would you like to be?

NOTES/THOUGHTS:

Day 186

Psalm 136:24 **Thank the Lord! He wears the badge of the Deliverer, he is compelled to, by his love.**—(iffy)

Questions:

Have you ever met someone whose integrity was like a sword and a shield?

Would you like to?

NOTES/THOUGHTS:

Day 187

Psalm 136:25 **Thank the Lord! His eternal purpose and intent is for each and every life.**
He calls us because he loves us!—(iffy)

Question:

Who cares for you eternally?

NOTES/THOUGHTS:

Day 188

Psalm 136:26 **His love sets things in order, takes into account all things, and his love isn't neglectful of any!**
Thank the Lord!—(iffy)

Questions:

What is your perception of justice? . . . Why?

What is your perception of lovingkindness? . . . Why?

NOTES/THOUGHTS:

Day 189

Psalm 139:23,24 **Search me, O God, and know my heart: try me, and know my thoughts:**
And see if there be any wicked way in me, and lead me in the way everlasting.—(AV)

Questions:

Can you afford to be really honest with yourself?

Will you get "hammered" if you totally open up?

NOTES/THOUGHTS:

Day 190

Proverbs 1:20-23 **Wisdom is not hidden, but stands in the open, her voice filters into everyplace.**
She is in the concourse of power and stands along the roads of commerce,
She can be heard in every corner of the city.
She says, "How long will you be so simple as to ignore your life?
How long will you make fun of others so as to avoid really living?
Why do you hate to know what can really set you free?
Listen to me!
And I will show you real life.
I will give you something to live for!—(iffy)

Question:

Are you walking in a fog?

Would you like to emerge with the sun shining down upon you?

NOTES/THOUGHTS:

Day 191

Proverbs 5:21 **There is nothing that a person does which escapes the Lord's attention; he ponders every step.**—(iffy)

Questions:

Is the idea of God watching you a liability? . . . Or could it be an asset?

NOTES/THOUGHTS:

Day 192

2 Corithians 4:6,7 **God commands the radiant light out
of darkness and, just like that, he brightens our
hearts, filling us so that we see God's glory as we
look into the face of Jesus Christ!
We're these clay pots, and we're brimming over
with this treasure!**—(iffy)

In ourselves there doesn't seem to be much.
We're just jars of clay, yet God dwells with us;
the treasure seen in our lives, his power.

Question:

What treasure do you have in your life, right now?

Do you think that you might have more than you know?

NOTES/THOUGHTS:

Day 193

Proverbs 9:1-6 **A house has been built by Wisdom,
it is supported by her seven pillars.
She has set the table within, and what there is to
eat and drink are by her hands.
Those that serve her are calling out, everywhere,
that her meal is being served by her, saying,
"Are you starving for answers yet always coming
up clueless?
But from Wisdom's hands is a feast of answers to
fill the vacuum of your uselessness: to give you
life and direction!
Please come."**—(iffy)

Question:

Are you hungry?

NOTES/THOUGHTS:

Day 194

Proverbs 10:3 **God's table is always ready for those who hunger after him.**
But the wicked person's cravings pushes God's hand away and finds starvation.—(iffy)

<u>Questions:</u>

Does failure stare you in the face?

Do you make the rules in your life?

NOTES/THOUGHTS:

Day 195

Proverbs 11:1 **God does not tolerate deceit and iniquity, but he rejoices in justice and consideration.**—(iffy)

Questions:

Does God appear to have "a world view"?

Would God's outlook have a place in your life?

Does your outlook make room for God?

NOTES/THOUGHTS:

Day 196

Proverbs 10:9 **The life committed to honesty and honor lives openly and in eternal safety.**
The fearful life of spin and lies will always be exposed.—(iffy)

<u>Questions:</u>

Are you a closed book?

Why?

NOTES/THOUGHTS:

Day 197

Proverbs 11:29 **He that troubleth his own house shall inherit the wind: and the fool shall be servant to the wise of heart.**—(AV)

<u>Questions:</u>

Have you ever been hurt and betrayed by someone close to you?

Is there anything you would like to do about it?

NOTES/THOUGHTS:

Day 198

Proverbs 12:20 **If a person thinks the worst in others, they wind up acting the same way; but joy is in the way of those who seek peace.**—(iffy)

Questions:

Do you suffer from paranoia?

Whether you do or not, do you think that there is a way out of that fog?

NOTES/THOUGHTS:

Day 199

Proverbs 14:30 **There is health to a heart and mind at peace.**
But destruction to the bones will find the person of ill will.—(iffy)

Question:

Are you holding onto, for dear life, things that are hurting you?

NOTES/THOUGHTS:

Day 200

Proverbs 15:1 **Anger is deflected by a tender response.**
But the acid tongue drops seeds of wrath and anger.—(iffy)

Questions:

What do you think of the person who excuses their behavior by saying, "Well, that's just how I am . . ."?

What kind of situations do you see that occuring in your life?

NOTES/THOUGHTS:

Day 201

Proverbs 15:25 **Pride, in all of its structures, won't be allowed to stand before God.**
On the other hand,
God personally lays the foundations of life for the most forsaken.—(iffy)

Questions:

Have you ever noticed instances of inequality in the world around you?

Is there a way to address those things?

NOTES/THOUGHTS:

Day 202

Proverbs 15:30 **The light of the eyes rejoiceth the heart: and a good report maketh the bones fat.**—(AV)

Questions:

Have simple words of encouragement given you a sense of comfort or hope?

If not, why not?

If they have, what were the circumstances?

NOTES/THOUGHTS:

Day 203

Proverbs 15:33 **Wisdom doesn't speak except through a deep reverence toward the Lord; consequently, it is only through real humility that we come upon high esteem and honor.**—(iffy)

Our paths can diverge,
yet the heart of love persists.
Sights along the path.

Question:

What, to you, is kindness and humility?

NOTES/THOUGHTS:

Day 204

Proverbs 16:2 **Our world and our plans extend to what we see, to what we sense.**
But God can measure the storm, and he can certainly see our motives.—(iffy)

Question:

Do you know the difference between what you desire and what you need?

NOTES/THOUGHTS:

Day 205

Proverbs 16:7 **Enemies are compelled to make peace with the person upon whom God's hands rest with his approval.**—(iffy)

<u>Question:</u>

Why are there enemies?

How can one always stay a friend?

NOTES/THOUGHTS:

Day 206

Proverbs 16:18 **Pride goeth before destruction, and an haughty spirit before a fall.**—(AV)

Questions:

When you think of the words "pride", "haughty"; and when you think of "better-than-thou" behavior, what mental images come to mind?

Do you have any particular feeling s about those images? . . . if you do, why?

NOTES/THOUGHTS:

Day 207

Proverbs 16:25 **There is a way that seemeth right unto a man, but the end thereof are the ways of death.**—(AV)

Questions:

How do you think such paths can be avoided?

Do you think that you've ever walked along such ways?

NOTES/THOUGHTS:

Day 208

Proverbs 17:14 **If you start a fight, there's no end of it until after the disaster; better to walk away.**—(iffy)

Questions:

What engages us to the battle? Ego? Hurt? Pride?

What about forgiveness and mercy?

NOTES/THOUGHTS:

Day 209

Proverbs 17:15 **God can't stand the person who applauds the sordid and the heartless, nor will he tolerate those who turn justice into an opportunity for denunciations.**—(iffy)

Question:

When someone turns your words against you, what does it do to you on the inside?

NOTES/THOUGHTS:

Day 210

Proverbs 17:20 **Unhappiness is the reward for the pitiless heart.**
And the person who says many things, but hides true intentions, will only find injury and resentment.—(iffy)

Questions:

Do you have a secret in your life that seems to be burning you from the inside out?

Are you consumed? . . . Or are you just tired?

NOTES/THOUGHTS:

Day 211

Proverbs 19:11 **Anger doesn't burn bright in the soul of a wise person whose brilliance comes through kindness and mercy.**—(iffy)

Question:

Do you have a fire in your heart?

Does it consume you, or does it heal you?

NOTES/THOUGHTS:

Day 212

Proverbs 20:22 **Don't say, "I'll have my revenge!"**
But, ultimately, God will take care of the problem
and he will help you.
Let the Lord take care of it all.—(iffy)

<u>Questions:</u>

How does one apply mercy?

Only when its easy?

NOTES/THOUGHTS:

Day 213

Proverbs 27:4 **The subversiveness of resentment and jealousy is more destructive than the malice of anger of the hurricane of rage.**—(iffy)

There is a hunger in wanting something.
At the core of your being, what is it?

Question:

What causes a person to want something?

Does that person want something good? . . . or does that person want something thought to be good?

NOTES/THOUGHTS:

Day 214

Proverbs 28:14 **Those that walk in awe and with kindness find eternal joy.**
Those that resist compassion stumble in a troublesome world.—(iffy)

Questions:

What do you think holds you back in your life?

What blesses you?

NOTES/THOUGHTS:

Day 215

Proverbs 29:23 **The natural order of arrogance is for the one who has it to eventually stumble and fall.**
Yet it's also the order of things that the one who walks in humility rises to be honored and celebrated.—(iffy)

Question:

Is there possibly an eternal virtue?

NOTES/THOUGHTS:

Day 216

Ecclesiastes 3:11 **Everything has a place of beauty in God's timing which sparks in us an unquenched sense of eternity.**
As the Lord moves we see him through a veil of mystery.—(iffy)

<u>Questions:</u>

Can you clear away the fog in your life?

Could God clear away the fog in your life?

NOTES/THOUGHTS:

Day 217

Ecclesiastes 7:13 **Consider the work of God: for who can make that straight, which he hath made crooked?**—(AV)

Question:

Can one intelligently question God's designs and patterns when one knows little or nothing of his intent or purpose?

NOTES/THOUGHTS:

Day 218

Isaiah 1:18 **God speaks to us, "Let's sit down and talk this out.**
   Your life is stained with your broken intentions; but I will transform it as white as snow.
   Though corruption has clotted the fibers of your life with dried blood;
   I will transform it to shimmer as lambs wool.—(iffy)

Whatever our attitude or status,
even when we're the lowest of the low,
God invites us to healing, to his love.

Question:

Can you deal with all the cards being on the table?

NOTES/THOUGHTS:

Day 219

2 Corinthians 5:1-3 **In our faith this is what we know: we find mortality in our bodies, dissolving with time; yet we have a God-built body that is eternal for a life in the heavens.**
Not wanting to be left alone, we've found home! Our very being is sheltered!
This is what we yearn for and desire.—(iffy)

The people find themselves raising their hands,
singing at sunrise and at waterfalls,
from somewhere deep, down inside a person.

Questions:

What is the true object of desire?

Is there a core expectation deeper and greater than we can celebrate?

NOTES/THOUGHTS:

Day 220

Isaiah 26:3,4 **Perfect peace resides in the mind of the person who is focused on you [God]; it is complete trust in you. The Holy One, the Lord, is eternally strong! Trust the Lord forever!**—(iffy)

Questions:

Where do your thoughts wander to?

Have you found a place of peace?

If you have, can you stay there?

NOTES/THOUGHTS:

Day 221

Isaiah 25:8 **Death will be consumed in God's victory!**
Any reason for the tears of sorrow will be erased by the Lord.
All the evil designs against his people will be blown away.
God's word will be brought into play!—(iffy)

Questions:

What if the reason for our fears were to be erased?

Could we go on with our lives without something to be afraid of?

How?

NOTES/THOUGHTS:

Day 222

Isaiah 40:31 **God gives strength to, and strengthens again, the people who watch and wait for him; those are the people who rise to every occasion, just like eagles, they pursue his purpose without weariness; they turn their backs on discouragement as they walk before the Lord.**—(iffy)

Questions:

Is there an indiscernable weight resting heavily upon your shoulders?

What are the options you have explored to be able to walk lightly?

NOTES/THOUGHTS:

Day 223

Isaiah 42:1-4 **[The Office of Christ]** **"Here is the Servant that I [God] set above all.**

He is imbued with my heart and my purpose, I am so happy with him because he will apply discernment and justice to all the people on earth!

But he will not try and draw attention to himself.

He will move with gentle care.

He will promote the flame of faith.

His justice will touch every life.

Every part of the earth will be waiting for his words, and he will never fail them, all will be turned to the way of the Lord!"—(iffy)

Questions:

Do you hunger for perfect justice?

Do crave perfect balance in your life?

NOTES/THOUGHTS:

Day 224

Isaiah 43:13 **Yea before the day was I am he; and
there is none that can deliver out of my hand:
I will work, and who shall let it?**—(AV)

Questions:

Do you feel locked in?

Are you locked in?

If someone were to have the keys of time, would you be
willing to talk to that person about being "locked in"?

NOTES/THOUGHTS:

Day 225

Isaiah 50:4 **It is the Lord God that makes me like a counselor, to be able to touch the weary soul with healing words, at the right time.**
God moves everyday. And everyday I awake to his words teaching me!—(iffy)

Questions:

If it were true that God calls, does he call us just to call us?

Or does he have something for us to do?

NOTES/THOUGHTS:

Day 226

Isaiah 55:6 **Seek ye the Lord while he may be found, call ye upon him while he is near.**—(AV)

God is always NOW.
NOW is the moment we live.
We have this moment.

Questions:

Does God seem far away? . . . could it be the other way around?

NOTES/THOUGHTS:

Day 227

Isaiah 55:8 **For my thoughts are not your thoughts, neither are your ways my ways, saith the Lord.**—(AV)

Questions:

Do you like it when people "put you in a box"?

Have you ever wondered what God might feel when people "put him in a box"?

NOTES/THOUGHTS:

Day 228

Isaiah 55:11 **[God words] "What I say doesn't return
    to my hearing like an echo. what I speak becomes
    action; it does, it becomes.
    The purpose that I speak returns,
    accomplished."**—(iffy)

Questions:

No matter how odd it seems, you know, those things that
God says? Could they be worth listening to from time to
time?

NOTES/THOUGHTS:

Day 229

Isaiah 56:3 **Neither let the son of a stranger, that hath joined himself to the Lord, speak saying,**
   The Lord hath utterly separated me from his people: neither let the eunuch say,
   Behold I am a dry tree.—(AV)

The Lord doesn't see
freaks, strangers and outsiders.
The Lord sees children.

Question:

Do you think that there is room for "mending" and "healing" in the process of belonging?

NOTES/THOUGHTS:

Day 230

Isaiah 64:8 **But now, O Lord, thou art our father; we are the clay, and thou our potter; and we are the work of thy hand.**—(AV)

Questions:

Could it be possible that God formed us? . . . each individually?

Could God, as well, have individual intentions for each of us?

NOTES/THOUGHTS:

Day 231

Isaiah 59:14,15 **Justice has been reversed. Goodness and honesty have been exiled because truth cannot be tolerated.**
The person of integrity is no longer welcome.
There is a vacuum of lies that drains the souls of truthseekers.
But now the Lord sees that there is no justice, and he clearly sees and he clearly displeased.—(iffy)

Questions:

Does morality and justice change?

Who, or what, decides when such things should change, if and when they do?

NOTES/THOUGHTS:

Day 232

Jeremiah 17:9,10 **The lies of the heart are matchless, it selfishly runs to the ruin of its owner. It is undependable.**
"I, the Lord, look into every heart.
I evaluate every thought.
I take the appropriate action for each person.
I am not fooled and I see the outworking of every deed, so that I will respond accordingly.—(iffy)

It is God who knows
the way the heart is designed.
No shadows in light.

Questions:

What keeps you on an even keel? . . . keeps you balanced so you don't fall down?

Do you have something or someone like that in your life?

NOTES/THOUGHTS:

Day 233

Jeremiah 22:16 **"Do you know what it means to know me?" asks the Lord.**
"When those in need and who are suffering find the leadership of their nation interceding in their behalf, then the nation will be blessed."—(iffy)

Questions:

What is the template for good conduct? Should it, does it, change from one person to a group of people?

Do you find that you've gotten lost in the shuffle?

NOTES/THOUGHTS:

Day 234

Lamentation 3:22-24 **It is of the Lord's mercies that we are not consumed; because his compassions fail not.**
They are new every morning; great is thy faithfulness.
The Lord is my portion, saith my soul; therefore will I hope in him.—(AV)

Questions:

Not seeing, yet believing; . . . is that faith at the end of a tether?

Still, is it possible to see the "new-ness" of compassion "every morning"?

NOTES/THOUGHTS:

Day 235

Psalm 139:16,17 **You saw me even as I was unformed. In your book is a whole accounting of my being, the blueprint of my becoming, but I was still a dream.**
   Yet those were your thoughts, O God; great in number and precious.—(iffy)

Questions:

What are you?

Who are you?

NOTES/THOUGHTS:

Day 236

Ezekiel 11:19-21 **"And to you who will serve me**
I will put in you a new heart and spirit;
what was cold and jagged will become a living
heart,
so that you can walk completely in my way.
We will have perfect communion with each other.
Those that choose the path that descends to
darkness
will find that it will fold down and crush them
with the weight of their own selfishness . . ."—(iffy)

Questions:

What do you think of when you think of "perfection"?

As well, how do you view "imperfection"?

How is either obtained? . . . if at all.

NOTES/THOUGHTS:

Day 237

Ezekiel 34:11,12 **For this is what God says,**
   "I will not only look for my sheep [you], I will find them [you].
   When a shepherd is with his sheep, even when they've been scattered all over the place, he looks for each and every one.
   I will do even more than that: even in the worst place, in the worst of times,
   I will find you and bring you home."—(iffy)

Questions:

Can you be reached by such uncompromising love?

If you can, how?

NOTES/THOUGHTS:

Day 238

Ezekiel 40:4 **And the man said unto me,**
Son of man behold with thine eyes, and hear
with thine ear, and set thine heart upon all that I
shall shew thee; for the intent that I shew them
unto thee art thou brought hither: declare all
that thou seest to the house of Israel.—(AV)

Questions:

What have you seen in your life?

Could you have seen messages from God with your eyes, but your heart filtered them out?

NOTES/THOUGHTS:

Day 239

Matthew 5:13 **Ye are the the salt of the earth; but if the salt has lost its savour, wherewith shall it be salted? it is thenceforth good for nothing, but to be cast out, and to be trodden under foot of men.**—(AV)

<u>Questions:</u>

What flavor are you?

Or have you lost your "savour"?

NOTES/THOUGHTS:

Day 240

Matthew 5:44 **"This is what I [Jesus] am telling you to do:**
You are to love your enemies; you are to speak with kindness to those who speak maliciously of you, even so much as to be genuinely loving to those who actively hate you; let those who are vindictive and manipulative experience the compassionate power of your prayers."—(iffy)

Questions:

Is this a call to radical behavior? . . . Can it work?

Why, or why not?

NOTES/THOUGHTS:

Day 241

Matthew 11:4-6 **Jesus answered and said unto them, Go and shew John again those which ye do hear and see:**
The blind receive their sight, and the lame walk, the lepers are cleansed, and the deaf hear, the dead are raised up, and the poor have the gospel preached to them,
And blessed is he, whosoever shall not be offended in me.—(AV)

Questions:

Could you live a life where you had nothing to hide?

If someone were to really look into you, what do you have to offer?

What do you think Jesus had to offer?

NOTES/THOUGHTS:

Day 242

Matthew 12:50 **For whosoever shall do the will of my Father which is in heaven, the same is my brother, and sister, and mother.**—(AV)

God sees our errors,
they are second to our needs.
Healing cleanses wrongs.

Questions:

Do you need to be needed?

Where is your family?

NOTES/THOUGHTS:

Day 243

Matthew 13;31,32 **Jesus offered another parable to his disciples.**

> **"This is like the kingdom of heaven: it's the smallest mustard seed. This seed has been planted by a farmer.**
>
> **This most insignificant of seeds will become the greatest of herbs; like a tree, even.**
>
> **And here come the birds of heaven to rest in its branches."**—(iffy)

Questions:

What is the most ignored part of "who you are"?

Could it be the most important part?

NOTES/THOUGHTS:

Day 244

Matthew 13:34,35 **And Jesus used parables with the crowds of people, he wouldn't speak to them without using parables.**
It was a prophesy fulfilled,
"I will speak in parables,
I will utter things which have been hidden since the foundation of the world."—(iffy)

Questions:

What lies hidden in your heart that even you can't figure out?

Could it be that this moment, right now, is a good time to find out?

NOTES/THOUGHTS:

Day 245

Matthew 16:24,25 **Jesus spoke to his disciples,**
   "If you are going to follow me you have to
   surrender your 'self' to me, then take up the
   humiliation of the cross and follow me.
   For if you reserve your soul for yourself, you will
   lose it.
   But if you surrender your soul for me, you will
   gain it."—(iffy)

Questions:

What is it that you hold onto in your sadness and in your despair?

What do you fear losing?

NOTES/THOUGHTS:

Day 246

Mark 15:35 **"You've left me in this terrible spot! Why Dad?"**—(iffy)

Questions:

Christ is on the cross in real pain, really alone . . . why are people just standing around and watching?

Is his cross our cross?

NOTES/THOUGHTS:

Day 247

Matthew 19:25,26 **Having heard him the astonished disciples asked,**
"Who is able to be saved?"
Jesus looked straight at them,
"Humanity can't save itself; but there are no impossibilities with God!"—(iffy)

Questions:

Do you feel isolated in your life? . . . in your endeavors?

Would you like company?

NOTES/THOUGHTS:

Day 248

Matthew 20:26-28 **"The way of the world is not the way of my followers, but whoever desires to achieve greatness must be everyone's servant.**
Whoever wants to standout must be a slave.
That is what the Son of Man, the Messiah, has done: he has come to serve, not be served: giving his life as a ransom for many."—(iffy)

Questions:

Is your greatest validation when someone loves you?

Who loves you?

NOTES/THOUGHTS:

Day 249

Matthew 20:31-34 **The crowd told the blind men to be quiet, but they still cried out to Jesus,**
Lord have mercy on us, son of David!"
And Jesus stopped what he was doing and he called over to them,
"What is it that you want me to do?"
They said, "We want to see."
And with compassion Jesus went over and touched their eyes.
They saw instantly . . . and followed him.—(iffy)

Questions:

Are you crying out in your heart?

Who's listening?

NOTES/THOUGHTS:

Day 250

Matthew 23:11,12 **"The greater of my disciples is the servant.**

Those that flaunt themselves will find themselves humbled.

But those who humble themselves will be exalted."—(iffy)

Questions:

A recurring theme set by Jesus; what does it tell you about him?

Does it pose any challenges for you?

NOTES/THOUGHTS:

Day 251

Matthew 24:42 **"Always pay attention, be on the lookout, your Lord is coming and you do not know when."**—(iffy)

<u>Questions:</u>

What do you keep an eye out for?

Is it for an opportunity that lasts forever?

NOTES/THOUGHTS:

Day 252

Mark 2:16,17 **When the religious lawyers and the very (very) religious saw Jesus sitting down to have a meal with the corrupt and the ungodly they said to his followers, "Why does he eat with the corrupt and the ungodly?"**
Jesus heard what they said and he responded,
"Healthy people don't need a doctor, sick people do.
I didn't come for 'perfect' people,
I came for those who need to turn from heart-sickness and error."—(iffy)

Questions:

If Jesus were waiting for you; would he be waiting for you to be perfect?

Or is he just waiting for you?

NOTES/THOUGHTS:

Day 253

Mark 6:34 **Is not this the carpenter, the son of Mary, the brother of James, and Joses, and of Juda, and Simon? and are not his sisters here with us?**
And they were offended at him. But Jesus said unto them,
A prophet is not without honour, but in his own country, and among his own kin, and in his own house.—(AV)

I know them quite well
and never bother with them.
Diamonds, rubies . . . bah!

Questions:

What have you learned, if anything, about what is sacred?

Have such things become so familiar that they're like images of decoration and furniture in your mind?

NOTES/THOUGHTS:

Day 254

Mark 7:6,7 **Jesus said to them [the very religious and the very critical],**

> **"Isaiah hit it dead on when he prophesied about your hypocrisy, as he said,**
> **'Here's a group of people who say nice things about me.**
> **But I [the Lord] am the last thing in their hearts. Their worship of me is an excuse to mislead others with their ideas, using my name.'"**—(iffy)

<u>Questions:</u>

Have you ever felt that you've been misled? . . . That there was something, or someone, standing between you and the truth?

NOTES/THOUGHTS:

Day 255

Mark 9:1 **Jesus said, "This is the truth;**
Some of you will see the kingdom of God before
you pass on.
And you will see it in its full power!"—(iffy)

Questions:

What is it that you expect from your life? . . . What are you
looking for?

NOTES/THOUGHTS:

Day 256

Mark 9:22,23 **"[From my son's childhood he's had this malignant force] it throws him into the fire and into the water to kill him, all the time.**
But if anything can be done to help us, have compassion on us."
"If anything can be done?" Jesus responded.
"For those who believe, all things are possible."—(iffy)

Questions:

Did what Jesus said sound like a formula? . . . or do we narrowly channel the possibilities in our lives?

NOTES/THOUGHTS:

Day 257

Mark 9:24 **The son's father responded to Jesus immediately, without hesitation.**
   "I do believe! But I need your help with my distrust and my fears!"—(iffy)

<u>Question:</u>

What is it that keeps you from healing hands and wholeness?

NOTES/THOUGHTS:

Day 258

Mark 9:49,50 **For every one shall be salted with fire, and every sacrifice shall be salted with salt.**
Salt is good: but if the salt have lost its saltness, wherewith will we season it?
Have salt in yourselves, and have peace with one another.—(AV)

Flavor in our lives.
Never bland, but exciting!
The savor of peace.

Questions:

How do you see your life unfolding as you look to the future?

How does the idea of "the salted life" reflect on the quality of your life, right now?

NOTES/THOUGHTS:

Day 259

Mark 10:17,18 **And Jesus began his journey, as he did a man ran up and bowed down to him.**
"Good Master! " he asked Jesus, "how do I get eternal life?"
But Jesus' response was, "Why are you calling me good?
God is good, there is none other."—(iffy)

Questions:

How do you look at Jesus?

How do you associate yourself with God? . . . or do you?

NOTES/THOUGHTS:

Day 260

Mark 10:31 **"But many that are first shall be last, and the last first."**—(iffy)

Questions:

How does Jesus' comment reflect upon achievement?

Or, perhaps, it should be asked: what does it say as far as our hopes for achievement?

NOTES/THOUGHTS:

Day 261

Mark 11:22,23 **And Jesus said to his followers,**
"Take possession of your faith in God. For the truth is that through faith a mountain rising in the sky can be dropped into the depths of the ocean.
If your heart has cast out fear and doubt, your words will not only ring true, they will manifest the truth; it will become."—(iffy)

Questions:

Can we (you, me) exist without the mediation of real truth?

How are you defined; by what is true, or by what you make the truth out to be?

NOTES/THOUGHTS:

Day 262

Mark 12:41-44 **And Jesus sat by the temple treasury and watched the people give; quite a few of the rich were very generous.**
But a poor widow gave only two cents.
And Jesus said to his followers,
"That widow over there gave more than all the others who've given.
For they gave a portion of much that they had; that poor woman put in everything that she had."—(iffy)

Questions:

Is it wealth when we have it? . . . or is it wealth when we give it?

What do you do with what you have?

Is your "wealth potential" closer than you think?

NOTES/THOUGHTS:

Day 263

Mark 13:31 **Heaven and earth shall pass away: but my words shall not pass away.**—(AV)

Imperfect words fade.
What is true embeds in stone.
Winds blow sand from rock.

Question:

Do you want something strong and enduring in your life?

NOTES/THOUGHTS:

Day 264

Luke 1:78,79 **Through the tender mercy of our God; whereby the dayspring from on high hath visited us, to give light to them that sit in darkness and in the shadow of death, to guide our feet into the way of peace.**—(AV)

A light to be seen
in darkest places, searching.
We look up, hopeful.

<u>Question:</u>

Where is the darkest place in your life, right now?

NOTES/THOUGHTS:

Day 265

Luke 5:21-25 **The religious lawyers and very (very) religious whispered, "This man says bad things. Who is he? Only God can forgive our mistakes, right?" But Jesus knew their secret reasonings and said, "Why don't you speak up? Is it easier to say, 'Your life's mistakes and errors are forgiven', or to say, 'Get up and walk'? You must learn that the Son of Man has power to forgive." So he told the paralyzed man, Get up! Take your bedroll and go home." And that man got up, took his bedroll and walked home, praising God all the way.**—(iffy)

The hurts of our lives
falter in the light of home.
The walk of the healed.

Questions:

If by a touch or a word you were healed of your pain, of your troubles, where where would you go? . . . what would you do?

Does your attitude, doubt or skepticism keep potential healing at arms length?

NOTES/THOUGHTS:

CONDUCT BECOMING . . . LUKE 6:27-38
(the Trail of Goodness)

Day 266

Luke 6:27,28 **"This is how you are to conduct yourselves, if you are willing to listen:**
Love your enemies; to those that hate you, do well and kindly by them; wish them well who wish you ill; those that treat you badly, intercede for their souls before God."—(iffy)

Questions:

Can you be kind to your enemy right out of the blue?

Or does something have to change in you? . . . If so, what?

NOTES/THOUGHTS:

Day 267

Luke 6:29 **"Those that punch you on one side of your face, let them punch you on the other.**
If they take your jacket, give them your shirt."—(iffy)

Questions:

Is it possible that hatred can be attacked by kindness? . . . That aggressive hostility can be defeated by aggressive generosity?

NOTES/THOUGHTS:

Day 268

Luke 6:30 **"Respond to requests with generous action; ask for nothing from the one who takes from you."**—(iffy)

Question:

Lender, creditor or servant, which provides the greatest opportunity?

NOTES/THOUGHTS:

Day 269

Luke 6:31 **"Treat others as you desire to be treated."**—(iffy)

Questions:

What speaks to your heart?

What calms your unease?

NOTES/THOUGHTS:

Day 270

Luke 6:32-34 **"What purpose does it serve if you love those who love you, exclusively? or if you just do good to those who do good to you? or if you give to someone with the expectation of getting something back?**
Any misguided person will do the same."—(iffy)

Question:

Could it be that a "new life" isn't about "new words", but of "new deeds" matching a whole new being?

NOTES/THOUGHTS:

Day 271

Luke 6:35,36 **"God the Father is merciful, you should follow his example:**
   Those enemies of yours? Love them.
   Do unconditional good.
   Don't expect a return from anybody because of your giving.
   God will take care of your reward very generously. You are his children?
   So follow him, he who is kind to the unthankful and the evil."—(iffy)

Of us God asks
is only what he will do.
We flow together.

Question:

Is goodness a one person act, or does it involve others?

NOTES/THOUGHTS:

Day 272

Luke 6:37 **"If you categorize people because of your prejudices, you'll find yourself judged in the same way.If you're ready to condemn people for their faults, you'll find yourself walking into the wall of your own condemnation.**
Forgiveness opens the door to your own forgiveness . . . and to freedom."—(iffy)

Mercy opens doors.
You build closets for grudges.
What's your house look like?

Question:

Is there room in your life for both bitterness and mercy?

NOTES/THOUGHTS:

Day 273

Luke 6:38 **"There is a cause and effect for the spirit of your actions.**

Giving with a good heart will be returned with even a greater measure; so that also strangers will touch you with their generosity."—(iffy)

<u>Question:</u>

What holds you back from doing good things?

NOTES/THOUGHTS:

Day 274

Luke 8:18 **Take heed therefore how ye hear: for whosoever hath, to him shall be given; and whosoever hath not, from him shall be taken even that which he seemeth to have.**—(AV)

Questions:

How do you listen?

Do you listen for what you want to hear? . . . or are you willing to listen to the rain falling, or the wind blowing.

NOTES/THOUGHTS:

Day 275

Luke 9:27 **But I tell you of a truth, there be some standing here, which shall not taste death, till they see the kingdom of God.**—(AV)

Question:

Could it be that when we truly pay attention we can discover the Kingdom before us?

NOTES/THOUGHTS:

Day 276

Luke 9:57,58 **And it came to pass, that as they went in
the way, a certain man said unto him,
Lord, I will follow thee whithersoever thou goest.
And Jesus said unto him,
Foxes have holes, and birds of the air have nests;
but the son of man hath not where to lay his
head.**—(AV)

Questions:

Why would one be drawn to live the life of Jesus?

Why might such a life appeal to you? . . . or not?

NOTES/THOUGHTS:

Day 277

Luke 10:3 **Go your ways: behold, I send you forth as lambs among wolves.**—(AV)

Questions:

If you were to be transformed, what direction do you think it would take you in?

What if you became a lamb?

NOTES/THOUGHTS:

Day 278

Luke 11:9,10 **"This is what I have to tell you:**
If you ask you shall get;
if you look for something, you'll find it;
knock on the door, then it will open.
Those that bother to ask, get.
Those that bother to look, find.
Those that bother to knock, are invited in."—(iffy)

Questions:

Are you afraid of the answer?

Are you afraid of what you might find?

Are you afraid of what is on the other side of the door?

NOTES/THOUGHTS:

Day 279

Luke 12:15 **Jesus said to those around him,**
   "You should know this; be on guard against envy
   want and greed.
   You must understand that abundant possessions
   are never equal to, or ever a part, of a person's
   life."—(iffy)

Questions:

Do you have a clear view of who you are?

Is there anything that keeps you from seeing clearly?

NOTES/THOUGHTS:

Day 280

Luke 12:34 **For where your treasure is, there will your heart be also.**—(AV)

Questions:

Where's your heart?

Is it in a place you would want to live in forever?

NOTES/THOUGHTS:

Day 281

Luke 12;51 **[Jesus said] "Do you think that I've come to bring peace in this world, as it is?**
Let me tell you something;
I'm here to bring conflict."—(iffy)

Question:

What do you think is the standard for "love" and "compassion"? . . . if there is one?

Is it possible that the pursuit of love and compassion will be resisted?

NOTES/THOUGHTS:

Day 282

Luke 14:12-14 **Then he [Jesus] said to his host,**
"When you're serving breakfast or your evening
meal, don't invite those you're close to, or your
rich friends, so that they can return the favor and
maybe even moreso.
But, and this is even better than that, make a feast
and invite the disadvantaged and the disabled.
Then you'll find true blessing!
You see, the disadvantaged and the disabled
can't return your generosity; yet when we're
raised to life again you will find a greater return
than you can imagine."—(iffy)

Questions:

Do we live our lives just to get things?

Do you live your life just to get things?

NOTES/THOUGHTS:

Day 283

Luke 17:20,21 **And the very (very) religious people
demanded that Jesus tell them when the kingdom
of God was coming.
He said, "You won't see the kingdom of God
coming.
It won't be 'Here it is!' or 'There it is!'
The kingdom of God is within you."**—(iffy)

Question:

Could it be that the answers to the questions and the
mysteries in your life are closer to you than you think?

NOTES/THOUGHTS:

Day 284

Luke 18:15-17 **Little children were brought to Jesus so that he could touch them.**
But his disciples tried to discourage those that were bringing them. In response Jesus said, "Let the little children come to me, don't stop them!
The kingdom of God belongs to them.
The ones that can't get into the kingdom of God are those who won't receive it like a little child does."—(iffy)

Castles are built to keep enemies out,
so they can't walk in and take us at rest,
when the door is closed and we are watching.
But one doesn't come into the kingdom
with a castle, but alone, as one is.

Questions:

Can you be as "care-less" as a little child?

Can you be as loving as a little child?

Have you constructed barriers around your life?

NOTES/THOUGHTS:

Day 285

John 3:7,8 **"You really shouldn't be surprised when I said, 'You must be reborn'.**
Think of the wind that blows in any direction.
You can hear it, but where it's coming from and where it's going you don't know.
Those born of the Spirit are like that."—(iffy)

Question:

So what's faith if it's not diving into the unknown?

NOTES/THOUGHTS:

Day 286

John 3:17,18 **"The Son wasn't sent by God to condemn the world.**

Salvation comes through the Son!

There is no condemnation for those who believe in the Son.

Condemnation is already in place for those who won't believe in the Son."—(iffy)

Questions:

When you're confronted with the facts of an issue, how do you respond to them?

How do you respond to facts that you're not comfortable with?

NOTES/THOUGHTS:

Day 287

John 3:16 **"His only Son was given by God because of his love for the world.**
There is no end or perishing for the believer of the Son, there's only eternal life!"—(iffy)

Questions:

Love! . . . what if it means the giving of everything most precious in your life?

Can you believe in that kind of love?

NOTES/THOUGHTS:

Day 288

John 3:21 **"There is this, that the one who acts according to the truth proceeds to the light, because truth is from God, so the deeds of that person will be revealed to all."**—(iffy)

<u>Questions:</u>

What kind of investment do you have in the things that you do?

How do you think others might perceive them?

NOTES/THOUGHTS:

Day 289

John 4:24 **God is a Spirit: and they that worship him must worship him in spirit and in truth.**—(AV)

<u>Question:</u>

If and when you go to a doctor to be seen, do you go for your opinion or for the doctor's opinion?

NOTES/THOUGHTS:

Day 290

John 6:35 **And Jesus said unto them, I am the bread of life: he that cometh to me shall never hunger; and he that believeth on me shall never thirst.**—(AV)

Questions:

Do you feel dry inside?

Are you hungry for something that you can't quite get a handle on?

If you do, why do you think that is?

NOTES/THOUGHTS:

Day 291

John 7:6 **Jesus said, "My moment hasn't come, but NOW is always your opportunity."**—(iffy)

Questions:

If you were to question "God", would you ask the same questions of yourself?

If you were to challenge "God", are you willing to take up the same challenge?

NOTES/THOUGHTS:

Day 292

John 8:51 **"I'm telling the truth in what I'm saying.
A person will never see death if what I say is kept
in the heart and used in life."**—(iffy)

Magic is a trick.
Miracles are from the heart.
Who walks on water?

<u>Question:</u>

Do you feel like you're just going through the motions in
your life?

NOTES/THOUGHTS:

Day 293

John 8:45 **"Because I tell you the truth, you choose the opposite way and won't believe me."**—(iffy)

Questions:

Can the truth hurt so much that you feel better if you ignore it? . . . or deny it?

If so, why?

NOTES/THOUGHTS:

Day 294

John 9:1-3 **Jesus walked by a man who'd been blind since the day he was born.**
"Master, teacher," asked his followers,
"did this guy transgress against God, or did his parents, so that he was born blind?"
However Jesus answered, "This isn't an issue of sin or error.
Here is where mercy is shown through what God does!"—(iffy)

Questions:

Do you look for the "bad" in problems? . . . or do you look for the "good"?

Is your perspective governed by what you see, or what you hear, or what you feel?

Is it possible that how you see things might be shaped by the condition of your heart?

NOTES/THOUGHTS:

Day 295

John 12:24,25 **"What I'm telling you now is a most important truth:**

A grain of wheat that doesn't die sits on the ground alone.

But when it's buried there is future fruit.

You should know that in grasping for your life it will slip away from you, it will be gone.

But the one who isn't content to find solace and comfort of life in this world shall find it in eternity!"—(iffy)

Question:

What do you see beyond this moment?

NOTES/THOUGHTS:

Day 296

John 13:34 **"Here's something I must say now. A command.**
A new one, as a gift to you.
You know I've loved all of you.
You need to translate that into love for each other.
Love one another!—(iffy)

Questions:

Is the idea of "universal love" just an idea and a good thought?

Could it be obtainable? . . . if so, how?

NOTES/THOUGHTS:

Day 297

Hebrews 6:18-20 **There are these unchangeable truths:**
One; God can't lie.
Two; because he can't lie, what he says stands with us.
We have fled from what we've known to a hope that is more real, because God has set it there.
So now we are anchored to what's beyond our vision, because Jesus has gone before us, passing through the unseen, our high priest, our Righteous King!—(iffy)

Questions:

Do you feel secure with the pain and discomfort that you've had to live with?

Yet does something call you to the invisible road? . . . toward a security you can't quite see?

NOTES/THOUGHTS:

Day 298

John 13:35 **"If you live and demonstrate love amongst yourselves all Humankind will see Christ-followers and what Christ-followers are."**—(iffy)

Question:

How elemental and basic in your life do you have to be to love? . . . to really love?

NOTES/THOUGHTS:

Day 299

John 14:12 **"What I'm saying to you is the truth.**
   Do you believe in me? That's good.
   But I'm going on to my Father.
   Yet the things that I have done you will also do.
   In fact you will do greater things."—(iffy)

Questions:

Do you live with decreased expectations for yourself? . . . and for others?

How is it, then, that Jesus expects that we might excel even him?

NOTES/THOUGHTS:

Day 300

John 14:27 **"Don't let your heart be filled with worry, or fear.**
The world can't give you what I'm giving you: peace!
I'm leaving you with peace . . . NOW!"—(iffy)

Questions:

Peace. World peace. Is there a difference?

Why do you think Jesus differentiates?

NOTES/THOUGHTS:

Day 301

John 15:4 **"Unless you stand in me what is the outcome**
of your life?
It's like a branch broken from a tree, no fruit.
Remain with me, I'll stay with you."—(iffy)

Questions:

What is the depth of Jesus statement? . . . his promise?

NOTES/THOUGHTS:

Day 302

John 15:13,14,17 **"A friend's life for a friend.**
 No one can show greater love than that.
 If you do what I tell you to do you are my friends.
 I command you to love one another."—(iffy)

Questions:

What actions in your life portray the essence of your character?

And how does your character stand in relationship with others?

NOTES/THOUGHTS:

Day 303

John 20:9 **His followers didn't understand the scriptures about him [Jesus] rising from the dead.**—(iffy)

<u>Questions:</u>

Does the "unknowable" scare you? . . . but could it be that you just don't know it, yet?

What does uncertainty do to your mindset?

NOTES/THOUGHTS:

Day 304

Acts 1:6-8 **The apostles were together with Jesus, and they asked him,**
"Lord, are you going to return to us the kingdom of Israel, right now?"
And he answered, "The times and the seasons are in the mind and power of the Father, it's not your concern.
This is how it will work:
When you are filled with the Holy Spirit you will receive power to confirm and validate my gospel in Jerusalem, in Judea and Samaria and to every corner of the world."—(iffy)

Questions:

What's the potential impact of simply "telling the truth"?

What would be the potential impact in your life if you were to act on the truth?

NOTES/THOUGHTS:

Day 305

Acts 1:14 **Now those folks prayed together and in agreement, humbly asking, imploring God for direction; the women disciples, as well as the men, Mary (Jesus' mother) and Jesus' brothers.**—(iffy)

Questions:

Prayer . . . is it possible that it's worth the time and effort? . . . for you?

NOTES/THOUGHTS:

Day 306

Acts 2:31,32 **"He [David the prophet/king] looked way beyond his time to Christ rising from the dead and the flesh of his body didn't decay.**
And we are witnesses that this very same Jesus was raised up again by God!"—(iffy)

Light swallows darkness.
Word of truth wove in action.
It has been foretold.

Questions:

Jesus rising from the dead? . . . what's best for you?

Why?

NOTES/THOUGHTS:

Day 307

Acts 3:2-8 **A man who was disabled at birth was carried everyday to the temple gate, which was called Beautiful, to beg for money. When he saw Peter and John walking into the temple he asked them for money, too. They both turned to him and Peter said, "Look at us." Expecting to get something from them he looked right at them. And then Peter said, "I don't have any money, but what I possess I will give to you. In the name of Jesus Christ, the Nazarene, get up and walk!" Peter took the man by his right hand and up he went, his feet and ankles immediately strengthened. Leaping, he stood and walked into the temple with Peter and John; walking, leaping and praising God.**—(iffy)

Questions:

Are you looking for answers? . . . or are you looking for solutions?

Do you want relief? . . . or do you want healing?

NOTES/THOUGHTS:

Day 308

Acts 3:14-16 **"Against God you refused the Holy One,
the Just One.
In his place you chose a murderer.
Your choice killed the Prince of Life.
But we've seen that God has restored him from
the place of death.
And that through faith in this same Holy One this
disabled man is now a whole man.
You all see him for yourselves."**—(iffy)

Love is flowing by
to be accepted by you.
Will your doors open?

Questions:

Does denying the truth make it any less truer?

And, where is the healing in "truth denial"? . . . or in "truth
acceptance"?

NOTES/THOUGHTS:

Day 309

Acts 3:19 **"Stop turning away from the divine, but allow yourselves to be transformed when the Lord comes to shower new life on all things!"**—(iffy)

Lost is forgetting.
Adventure is remembrance.
It is in the choice.

Question:

The truth may hurt and be painful; but is that the sole purpose of truth?

NOTES/THOUGHTS:

Day 310

Acts 4:9-11 **"This man has been healed.**
How did this happen to a disabled person?
I suppose this good deed is why we're being
questioned here.
I certainly don't want to conceal the truth form
all the people of the nation:
It is by the name of Jesus the Nazarene; whom
you executed; whom God raised from death.
It is by this Jesus that this man, once crippled, is
now whole!
You builders ignored the stone that enables the
building!"—(iffy)

Nothing is hidden
in the gospel mystery.
Will we see, or not?

Question:

Can wholeness and healing, when it's out of a "controlled"
setting, open up a can of worms?

NOTES/THOUGHTS:

Day 311

Acts 4:12 **"Can souls be rescued, or salvaged, or redeemed by any other [but Jesus Christ]? No. There is no other name under heaven given for the saving of humanity."**—(iffy)

Questions:

This statement was addressed to a religious "expert"; do you think there can be conflicts between "experts" and understanding?

If there are, how can this be?

NOTES/THOUGHTS:

Day 312

Acts 4:13,14 **At the moment of Peter's and John's audacity the priests and their religious lawyers had understood these men to be uneducated and untrained, though they did know they'd been with Jesus.**
But in their wonder they still couldn't argue the point:
There was the healed man standing with Peter and John.—(iffy)

Questions:

Would you allow yourself to be convinced of the truth, no matter how painful and awkward, if it stood in front of you?

Or, would you allow your prejudices, hurts and dislikes to reject what is irrefutable? . . . if so, why?

NOTES/THOUGHTS:

Day 313

Acts 9:4,5 **Saul fell to the ground and a voice addressed him.**

"Saul, Saul, why are you persecuting me?"

And Saul asked, "Who are you, sir?"

And the Lord responded, "I am Jesus, the one you're persecuting.

It's hard for you to kick against the thorns, isn't it?"—(iffy)

Question:

In your despair and in your anger do you lash out against those who love you the most?

NOTES/THOUGHTS:

Day 314

Acts 16:22-30 **The crowd in the marketplace opposed Paul and Silas.**

So the judges of the city had them stripped and beaten.

They were then turned over to the sheriff, who was told to imprison them securely.

Their feet were fastened to the floor in the heart of the prison.

So there were Paul and Silas at midnight, praying and singing to God while the other prisoners listened.

Suddenly there was an earthquake so great it shook all the prison doors open and the prisoners' shackles were broken.

The sheriff was shaken awake.

He immediately saw that all the doors to the prison were hanging, wide open.

He drew his weapon to kill himself.

"Don't do anything stupid! We're all in here!" Paul shouted to the sheriff.

The sheriff got the lights on and fell down before Paul and Silas, trembling.

"Sirs, what must I do to be saved?", he asked, as he brought them out of prison.—(iffy)

Questions:

Are you prepared for circumstances to be changed in your life?

Have you thought about preparing for circumstances to be changed in your life?

NOTES/THOUGHTS:

Day 315

Acts 16:31 **Paul and Silas told the sheriff,**
   "Believe in Jesus Christ the Lord, then you'll be
   saved, and your family will be saved."—(iffy)

Questions:

What are the decisions set before you right now?

Could they effect other people, too?

NOTES/THOUGHTS:

Day 316

Acts 17:22,23 **Paul was standing before the Mars Hill council and said,**
> **"I see, Athenians, how very fearful of gods you are.**
> **Passing through and looking at all of your shrines**
> **I also found this one particular altar; written on it are the words, 'To The Unknown God'.**
> **Who you do not know in your worship, this is the One I am presenting to you."**—(iffy)

Something is out there
beyond our understanding.
Why are we afraid?

Question:

Are you content with the UNKNOWN when it is available to be KNOWN?

NOTES/THOUGHTS:

Day 317

Matthew 19:21 **To the young man Jesus said,**
Come and follow me, you will have eternal
treasure after you give to those in desperate
need from all your possessions which you should
sell off."—(iffy)

Questions:

Perfection . . . where is it in what Jesus said? . . . or is it
there at all?

NOTES/THOUGHTS:

Day 318

Romans 1:19,20 **We don't have an excuse to ignore God, really, because it's true that much of what can be known of him is shown in our lives.**
It is God who has revealed it to us; his being, who he is, his total mastery of eternity are to be seen by all his children.
Those things that have been invisible since the beginning are to be understood by us.—(iffy)

Questions:

What do you think is hidden in plain sight?

Why do you think that this is so?

NOTES/THOUGHTS:

Day 319

Romans 5:6-8 **Unknowingly, we've been in a state of total helplessness.**
(And we were out of control.)
It was at this moment of spiritual bankruptcy that the sacrifice of Jesus' life was made for us.
I mean barely anyone would be willing to do this for a really good and holy person.
And, maybe, there's even a few who would do this for someone who's just getting by.
But God's love proves itself by Christ dying for us at our worst.—(iffy)

Questions:

When someone gives up something for our benefit, is that effort worth our attention?

Could it be worth looking into?

NOTES/THOUGHTS:

Day 320

Romans 6:11 **Likewise ye also yourselves to be dead unto sin, but alive unto God through Jesus Christ our Lord.**—(AV)

Death leads us to life
through the pain of another.
Falseness left behind.

Questions:

Can you be in "control" and still be "alive"?

Can your life be had through another's death?

NOTES/THOUGHTS:

Day 321

Romans 6:23 **Jesus, the Lord of us, gives us, free of charge, eternal life.**
   But if we choose error and defiance we must work for it, and its payment is death.—(iffy)

Questions:

How in it that we have such a hard time is seeing such things this clearly?

Or, is it really that simple?

NOTES/THOUGHTS:

Day 322

Romans 8:1 **Who walks in the Spirit?**
Well, it's for certain they've walked away from transgression and condemnation and guilt; they've walked into Jesus Christ!—(iffy)

To turn away from . . .
is to turn and face into.
Eternity beckons!

Questions:

Where does your mind take you at the end of the day? . . . where would you like it to be?

NOTES/THOUGHTS:

Day 323

Romans 8:14,15 **The children of God are led by the Spirit of God.**
And we comfortably call him "Dad", for we no longer live in fear and in slavery, but in the Spirit of holy adoption.—(iffy)

Questions:

Is there something "going on in your life"?

Do you have an underlying feeling, a sense, that you suffer on a daily basis?

NOTES/THOUGHTS:

Day 324

Romans 8:38,39 **What is in the Lord Jesus Christ?**
I've become absolutely convinced that nothing, not death, not life, not angels, not nations, not spiritual dominions, not current problems, not the doom just over the horizon, nothing "high and noble", nothing "low and degrading", there is nothing in creation that will ever separate us from what is in Jesus, and that is the love of God!—(iffy)

Questions:

Do you live in this equation? . . . or on the the outside of it?

NOTES/THOUGHTS:

Day 325

Romans 10:13 **For whoever shall call upon the name of the Lord shall be saved.**—(AV)

Turning the light on
ends our fears of stumbling.
Darkness disappears.

Question:

Do you think that a decision made is like "flipping on a switch"?

NOTES/THOUGHTS:

Day 326

Romans 10:17 **So does faith come by itself?**
   It comes by hearing.
   And what is it that we hear?
   We hear living words coming from God.—(iffy)

<u>Questions:</u>

Does your set of beliefs connect with something? . . . or someone?

NOTES/THOUGHTS:

Day 327

Romans 12:2 **What is good and acceptable to God? It's certainly not in conformity to this world; but, rather, it is by allowing your mind and your heart to be perfectly renewed in his will.**—(iffy)

Questions:

Are you a good citizen?

And if you are, what are you a citizen of?

NOTES/THOUGHTS:

Day 328

Romans 12:20,21 **Good overcomes evil.**
  **Good conduct is our defense against evil conduct.
  Conviction is laid in the heart and in the mind of
  your enemy when you give them a meal when
  they're hungry; when you give them something
  to drink when they're thirsty.
  Overcome evil with good.**—(iffy)

Look beyond anger,
discover a world of need.
Don't smother God's love.

Questions:

Can the energy of anger sustain you?

What can possibly keep you going for eternity?

NOTES/THOUGHTS:

Day 329

1 Corinthians 2:14-16 **The so-called independent person (who's really just independent from God) cannot accept the things of God, they are foolishness for a person determined to ignore the Spirit of God. But the person who can appraise the spiritual is an enigma to those who turn their back on God. Because, as Isaiah says,**
"Who knows the mind of the Lord, that he may be taught?"
Well, Christ knows the mind of God; we're enigmatic because we know Christ!—(iffy)

Questions:

Are you clueless?

Do you choose to clueless? . . . or is that choice knocking at your door?

NOTES/THOUGHTS:

Day 330

1 Corinthians 4:3,4 **The truth is that the value of what any person thinks of me isn't my concern.**
Really, I don't know of anything I've done wrong.
Yet I still could be guilty of something really bad.
Only God truly and clearly sees me for who I am.—(iffy)

Questions:

When you have self-doubt do you find that all your questions just lead to more questions and uncertainties?

Are living in an endless, self-consuming, circular file?

NOTES/THOUGHTS:

Day 331

1 Corinthians 8:2,3 **Do you see the "know-it-all"?**
That person's usually clueless.
But here's how that person should find his answers:
Love God.
God knows that man . . . and that is
enough.—(iffy)

Questions:

What is the one core thing in your life you feel that you need in order to survive?

Can you get it?

Can you hold onto it?

NOTES/THOUGHTS:

Day 332

1 Corinthians 11:1 **Follow me as I follow Christ.**—(iffy)

<u>Question:</u>

What is the most simple thing about a path?

NOTES/THOUGHTS:

THE PERSONALITY OF FAITH
(The Love Chapter . . . 1 Corinthians 13)

Day 333

1 Corinthians 13:1 **([1 Corinthians 12:31b] Still, I'm
going to show you the best way; here it is:)
Even if I could speak all the languages of the
world and of the angels, but did so without love,
I would, at best, be making uncertain
sounds.**—(iffy)

Questions:

Have you ever listened to an eloquent sounding speech and
forgot what it was about?

Have you ever heard a gut-wrenching cry that pierced your
heart?

NOTES/THOUGHTS:

Day 334

1 Corinthians 13:2 **And even if I had the ability to forecast into the future, to explain the unexplainable, to be knowledgeable in everything, to be able to remove every natural obstacle, yet found myself unable to love,**

I would be, literally, nothing.—(iffy)

Question:

Have you ever had your expectations met and still felt alone and sad in the end?

NOTES/THOUGHTS:

Day 335

1 Corinthians 13:3 **And even if I am the most giving and charitable person, sacrificing my possessions and laying down my life for the cause of the poor and forgotten, but do not have love, it becomes, all of it, an empty and futile gesture.**—(iffy)

Questions:

Are you going through the motions?

Does something need to change?

NOTES/THOUGHTS:

Day 336

1 Corinthians 13:4 **This is the kind of love I'm speaking of:**
It is the love that doesn't surrender and yet maintains an attitude of enduring kindness.
It is the kind of love that refuses to envy others for their joy and successes; but would rather rejoice with them and support them in their happiness.—(iffy)

Question:

Could your love and humility become a source of strength for others?

NOTES/THOUGHTS:

Day 337

1 Corinthians 13:5 **This is the kind of love that has a graceful heart which transforms our graceless nature so that we're content, even with strangers.**
It's the love that extends kindness in the face of hostility and looks for the best in the worst.—(iffy)

Questions:

Could you consider this pattern of conduct?

Would you be able to receive this kind of love?

NOTES/THOUGHTS:

Day 338

1 Corinthians 13:6 **This is the love that refuses to see the bright side of any evil deed, yet is joyful in the light of all the facets of the truth.**—(iffy)

Question:

Can love for the truth be an honest path of discovery?

NOTES/THOUGHTS:

Day 339

1 Corinthians 13:7 **This is the love that carries the burden.**
This is the love that sees through the haze, that blinds the skeptic, and opens the door to hope; it's why love, this love, will endure.—(iffy)

Questions:

Is the distant spark of hope you have seeming to fade?

Is your heart broken?

Does it need to be broken?

NOTES/THOUGHTS:

Day 340

1 Corinthians 13:8 **Does this love ever fail?**
No!
But prophesy, which points to an end, will; and so will be finished of its work.
The encouragement that comes with spiritual and earthly language will fall silent.
And knowledge will vanish.—(iffy)

Question:

What kind of love keeps on going when other transcendent landmarks seem to fade away?

NOTES/THOUGHTS:

Day 341

1 Corinthians 13:9,10 **Our knowledge is incomplete and prophesy shows us where we aren't, so that what is incomplete will no longer have use when "perfect" has come.**—(iffy)

Question:

How could love get us ready for the perfect?

NOTES/THOUGHTS:

Day 342

1 Corinthians 13:11-13 **Just like in my childhood**
   I could only speak of what I could grasp and understand with the thought precesses of a child; in adulthood those thought processes had been replaced.
   So, now, our vision is, at best, dim.
   In the future we have absolute clarity.
   Now, my knowledge is incomplete.
   Then, I will know completely even as I am completely known.
   But there are those three which abide with us and endure:
   Faith, hope and love.
   The greatest of these?
   Love!—(iffy)

Questions:

Can you, can I, even get near this love? . . . if so, how?

NOTES/THOUGHTS:

Day 343

Galatians 3:27,28 **For as many of you as have been baptized into Christ have put on Christ; there is neither Jew nor Greek, there is neither bond nor free, there is neither male nor female: for ye are all one in Christ Jesus.—(AV)**

Questions:

There always seem to be questions of exclusiveness and inclusiveness . . . what's your read on the issue?

What do you think [the writer] Paul's was?

NOTES/THOUGHTS:

Day 344

Ephesians 2:8,9 **It is by God's radical, unremitting favor
that salvation has come to us by faith; we didn't
do it.**
It is God's gift.
We didn't work to make salvation happen.
**Humanity didn't enable GRACE; but we are
definitely invited in.**—(iffy)

Question:

If God holds a gift out to you, for you . . . would you take
it?

NOTES/THOUGHTS:

Day 345

Ephesians 5:1,2 **Be ye therefore followers of God, as dear children; and walk in love, as Christ also hath loved us, and hath given himself for us an offering and sacrifice to God for a sweet smelling savour.**—(AV)

Questions:

Sacrifice?

What can one possibly return for another's sacrifice?

NOTES/THOUGHTS:

Day 346

Philippians 1:21 **For to me to live is Christ, and to die is gain.**—(AV)

Questions:

What is, do you think, the "culture of Christ"; is it simply a philosophy?

Is it an internalized lifestyle?

Is it more? . . . or less?

NOTES/THOUGHTS:

Day 347

1 Thessalonians 3:12 **Let the Lord Jesus cause your love to grow and spread out to not only love your brothers and sisters, but the whole of humanity. This is the quality of love we have for you.**—(iffy)

Questions:

What invites and entices you to kind and generous action?

What holds you back from kindness and generosity?

NOTES/THOUGHTS:

Day 348

1 Thessalonians 5:16-18 **What is the will of God?**
   Always, always, rejoice!
   Never stop talking to him!
   In every part of your life be thankful!
   **This is the pattern of Christ Jesus for your
   life.**—(iffy)

Questions:

Right now . . . how would you define your life?

Are there dimensions of it that you need to change? . . . if
so, what? . . . how?

NOTES/THOUGHTS:

Day 349

Hebrews 2:9 **But we see Jesus who, by God's favor, tasted death for every man, woman and child. Jesus (lowered below all angelic orders) ascended from death to be crowned with glory and honor.**—(iffy)

Question:

If (and this is a big "if") Jesus did this, why not follow him?

NOTES/THOUGHTS:

Day 350

Hebrews 4:7 **"Today!" is the time he gave and spoke to David the king.**
And throughout all time "Today!" is for those who will open their hearts and listen to God.—(iffy)

Questions:

This moment, right now . . . are you guaranteed anything more than that? . . . more than what you have here, today?

NOTES/THOUGHTS:

Day 351

Hebrews 9:28 **In Christ all the mistakes and errors of mankind have been sacrificed; and so with salvation, and free of transgression, we will look for this exact same Christ,**
for a second appearance.—(iffy)

Question:

What do you have to look for ward to if something is always keeping you back?

NOTES/THOUGHTS:

Day 352

James 1:19,20 **The anger of man doesn't demonstrate the completeness and wholeness of God.**
   So anger should be the very last thing you show in your life.
   Speaking your mind should be next to the last on your list.
   But let us be attentive to listen, demonstrating the love of our fellowship.—(iffy)

I am left helpless,
my armor is made useless.
Leaves fall in Autumn.

Questions:

Is this permission for good conduct?

Do you need permission?

NOTES/THOUGHTS:

Day 353

James 2:5 **Look at this, my fellow Christ-followers; God has intentionally picked the lowliest in this world to have the richest faith; these are the ones he has promised the kingdom, the ones who love him.**—(iffy)

Questions:

Where is the church?
Have you looked in the streets?
Have you looked at the espresso bar?
Have you looked where you go shopping?
Have you looked outside your door? . . . inside?
Have you looked in the mirror?

NOTES/THOUGHTS:

Day 354

James 5:19,20 **I want you to know something, my fellow Christ-followers:**
If one of you wanders from the truth, but another persuades him back, that is the daily scale of the gospel life.
It is that simple loving action that covers a multitude of sins.—(iffy)

<u>Question:</u>

Why do you think James ends his letter with this simple point?

NOTES/THOUGHTS:

Day 355

1 Peter 5:6,7 **We are in the care of our mighty God, who will raise us to full joyousness and acknowledgement.**
Now let us walk humbly, laying our cares in his hands as he always cares for us.—(iffy)

Questions:

Do you feel alone?

Are you invited?

NOTES/THOUGHTS:

Day 356

2 Peter 3:8 **But, beloved, be not ignorant of this one thing, that one day is with the Lord as a thousand years, and a thousand years as one day.**—(AV)

Less than a moment,
he is closer than a thought.
Always and always.

Questions:

Where do you go in your quiet moments? . . . who keeps you company?

NOTES/THOUGHTS:

Day 357

1 John 1:5 **The message that we received from Jesus,
who spoke to us, we're passing on to you:
God is light! There is no place of darkness in him,
none!**—(iffy)

Question:

What is true and dependable in your life?

NOTES/THOUGHTS:

Day 358

1 John 2:25 **And this is the promise that he [Jesus] hath promised us, even eternal life.**—(AV)

Questions:

Is there more to "eternal life" than just longevity?

Will you hope for what you can't see?

Can you surrender to the unseen?

NOTES/THOUGHTS:

Day 359

Luke 10:38-42 **Jesus and his followers visited a particular town. And in this town they were guests at the house of a woman named Martha. Martha had a sister, Mary, who sat and listened to all that Jesus taught. But Martha was so busy with the chores of entertaining that she had no time to sit and to listen. During a pause Martha complained to Jesus about Mary not helping her:**
"Lord, don't you care? Tell Mary to help me?"
"Boy, Martha!" Jesus responded, "You have a lot of things going on.
But Mary's doing only one thing, for sure.
Fortunately for her, it's the one thing that's really important."—(iffy)

Questions:

If you were to trim down the things in your life that weren't essential, would you find it difficult?
What one thing is the most important to you?

NOTES/THOUGHTS:

Day 360

Isaiah 29:13,14 **And God said, "These people say nice things about me.**

Why, they identify with me, sort of.

Because, really, their hearts are given to someone, or something, else.

What respect they might have for me is through their rule books, through their religion.

So I will have to show them, quite dramatically, that their philosophical structures, their attempts at bringing faith under control, are wasted energy; that their theology and their understanding really make no sense at all."—(iffy)

Questions:

Are you trying to build bridges?

Do you have any idea what's on the other side?

Are you interested?

NOTES/THOUGHTS:

Day 361

John 8:32 **And ye shall know the truth, and the truth shall make you free.**—(AV)

Questions:

Truth, freedom . . . do you think it's really that simple? . . . why, or why not?

How do you think that truth and freedom might relate to each other?

What is freedom to you?

NOTES/THOUGHTS:

Day 362

Psalm 38:9-11 **You've seen all that I've longed for and desired, oh God.**
You know the groans of my disappointment.
My heart is racing as my knees buckle.
Sorrow is all that I see before me.
Those that loved me, my friends and closest associates, are somewhere else;
I haven't seen them for some time.—(iffy)

Questions:

Why does this person talk to, write to, God when he's apparently so down?

Can you relate to him?

If you can; is there anything that "snaps you out of it"?

NOTES/THOUGHTS:

Day 363

Psalm 142:4,5 **All my close friends disappeared.**
   I became homeless and was forgotten.
   That's when I turned to you, oh Lord!
   You are the place I want to be.
   Through what I've lost
   I found what I desire the most!—(iffy)

Questions:

Can you think of the most uncomfortable and awkward situation that you've ever been in? . . .

. . . Did anything good come of it?

NOTES/THOUGHTS:

Day 364

Luke 24:15-17 **Now these two disciples talked about all that had happened, trying to figure it all out. As they walked along, Jesus joined them. But they couldn't recognize him. He was like a stranger to them. So he asked, "What's all this stuff you're talking about? You appear to be walking under a cloud of sadness."**—(iffy)

Questions:

What "ingredient" do you think would make your life a better one?

Could the right ingredient be closer than you think?

NOTES/THOUGHTS:

Day 365

1 Corinthians 14:15 **Here's what I'm going to do: I will pray through with God's Spirit and in partnership with understanding; and I will sing with God's Spirit as I walk in comprehension of him; and as I walk with those around me.**—(iffy)

Questions:

Is there a song in your heart?

If there is, is that song for just a place? . . . an occasion? . . . or is it for your whole life?

NOTES/THOUGHTS:

Day 366

1 Timothy 1:5 **Now here is the goal of good instruction:**
Pure love from a clean heart; a conscience that's sound through and through; and a pure faith.—(iffy)

Question:

If you were to see yourself clearly . . . what do you think you'd look like?

NOTES/THOUGHTS: